MIND OVER GOLF

MIND OVER
GOLF

PLAY YOUR BEST BY THINKING SMART

DR. RICHARD H. COOP

WITH

BILL FIELDS

MACMILLAN PUBLISHING COMPANY
NEW YORK

MAXWELL MACMILLAN CANADA
TORONTO

MAXWELL MACMILLAN INTERNATIONAL
NEW YORK OXFORD SINGAPORE SYDNEY

Copyright © 1993 by Dr. Richard H. Coop and Bill Fields

Macmillan Publishing Company
866 Third Avenue
New York, NY 10022

Maxwell Macmillan Canada, Inc.
1200 Eglinton Avenue East
Suite 200
Don Mills, Ontario M3C 3N1

Macmillan Publishing Company is part of the Maxwell Communication Group
of Companies.

Library of Congress Cataloging-in-Publication Data

Coop, Richard.
    Mind over golf / Richard H. Coop with Bill Fields.
        p.   cm.
    Includes index.
    ISBN 0-02-527830-4
    1. Golf—Psychological aspects.   I. Fields, Bill.   II. Title.
GV979.P75C66   1993   92-20575   CIP
796.352'01—dc20

Macmillan books are available at special discounts for bulk purchases for sales
promotions, premiums, fund-raising, or educational use. For details, contact:

Special Sales Director
Macmillan Publishing Company
866 Third Avenue
New York, NY 10022

10 9 8 7 6 5

Printed in the United States of America

Design by Diane Stevenson / SNAP·HAUS GRAPHICS

To my parents, Paul and Sara Coop. They were both teachers who taught me to value and respect the process of teaching and learning.

Contents

ACKNOWLEDGMENTS

This book has been in progress for the past seventeen years, during which time I have worked with more than 700 golfers—from tour players to high-handicappers—on the mental side of golf. I have accompanied golfers to all four of the major championships and have shared their expectations, frustrations, and exhilarations as they competed at the highest level of the sport. At the other end of the spectrum, I have worked with beginning golfers who were just learning the fundamentals. I've also had the opportunity to teach in golf schools with the most respected instructors in the game and have talked with them privately about the golf swing in particular and the game of golf in general. From each of these people and situations I have had the chance to learn something more about how the mind works on the golf course.

This practical experience has been combined with my formal training in educational and sports psychology, cognitive behavior modification, social psychology, attribution theory, and biomechanics to produce this book. To each of these tour players, golf school students, and instructors I express my deepest gratitude.

Since 1986, I have had the good fortune of writing a continuing column for *Golf Illustrated.* In writing for the magazine, I have had to sharpen and order my thoughts on the mental side of golf in order to communicate to its readers. Some of the material which I originally conceptualized for these articles is found in this book. I thank my editors at *Golf Illustrated,* Al Barkow and Mike Corcoran, for giving me the opportunity over the years to address a wide audience of golfers.

I am also indebted to Bill Fields, who collaborated on this book with me, for helping me express my thoughts in a more readable manner than the awkward academic format to which I was accustomed. His editorial skills are much appreciated. Rick Wolff, my editor at Macmillan Publishing Company, has provided enthusiastic support and encouragement throughout the book's development. It is a wonderful circumstance that Rick is a practicing sports psychologist himself as well as an editor. His suggestions have been consistently helpful and on target.

A special acknowledgment is due to two people, Payne Stewart and Chuck Cook, who began as my professional associates and have developed into close personal friends. The sharing of experiences, both highs and lows, makes life worthwhile, and I have shared both good times and bad with these two men.

The most important acknowledgment, however, is to my family: my wife, Sharon, my daughters, Kristy and Kelli, and my son, Daniel. They have tolerated and supported my absences from them (sometimes even when my body was physically present) in order that I might gain the knowledge on which this book is based. Without them, it would not have been possible, and I thank them for their patience.

Richard H. Coop
Chapel Hill, North Carolina
July 1992

Having known Dick Coop for more than four years now, as a teacher of the mental side of golf, and as a good friend, it's a pleasure to contribute this introduction to a book that should help you improve your game and also enjoy it more.

Although people always have talked about how mental a game golf is, if you're like I was until I began working with Dr. Coop back in 1988, you probably don't understand what a sound mental approach to golf is all about. In my case, I seemed to have had all the physical tools to attain some big goals in golf, yet I had only a couple of wins and a bunch or runner-up finishes to show for my efforts. Everyone—myself included—thought I should have been accomplishing more, and the fact that I hadn't done so was both frustrating and disappointing.

I admit it: I was reluctant to seek Dr. Coop's help at first. I thought working with a psychologist would involve lying down on a couch and having a weird guy ask me a lot of questions. But nothing could have been further from the truth. After just one afternoon and the following morning of talking with Dick, I felt better about my golf game and about myself, and we've built on those sessions ever since.

My game always had seemed to get me into position to win, but I didn't have what it took to allow me to capitalize on the position I was getting in. I was too interested in the end result of winning—and not enough in the process that I had to go through in order to achieve my goals. Dr.

Coop helped me relax and let my swing take over. He encouraged me to develop a consistent preshot routine and use it whether it's my first swing on Thursday morning or the last one on Sunday afternoon, when the pressure of competition is at its greatest.

Proof that my game has matured since I began working with Dr. Coop were my victories in the 1989 PGA Championship and the 1991 U.S. Open. With my old mind-set, I don't think I would have been able to prevail in either of those major championships. But with my new mental approach, I was able to raise my game to the highest level when I had to.

I won't kid you—improving my mental fundamentals wasn't easy. In fact, one of the first things I had to get through my head—and you will, too, if you are to improve—is that ingraining a sound psychological approach to your game can take as much effort as retooling your swing mechanics. In fact, it can take more of an effort.

But trust me, the effort will be worth it. If you're a low-handicap golfer already, Dr. Coop's instruction can enable you to take advantage of your physical skills and move ahead to the next level, as I was able to do. If your game lacks some physical skills, learning the proper mental approach can help compensate for—but won't erase—the deficiencies in your swing. For all of the strange swings I see week to week in pro-ams on the PGA Tour, I see just as many—or more—errors committed on the mental side. Not everyone can swing like a tour pro, but most everyone has it within himself or herself to begin to think like one, and Dr. Coop lays the foundation for that within these pages.

FOREWORD

My hope for you is that his advice will help your game as much as it has helped mine. Good luck, and good golfing.

—Payne Stewart

THE REASON
FOR THIS BOOK

If you've paid much attention to professional golf over the last several years, you've probably heard about how sports psychologists have helped some of the sport's best players improve their games. You might be wondering what really goes on between the players and the sports psychologists, and what their lessons could mean to you. Could learning how to think more appropriately on the course actually help you more than yet another visit to your local driving range to slug out another bucket of balls?

The answer, as I hope to make clear in these pages, definitely is yes. Like the finest players in golf, you can also improve your game by paying attention to the mental side of golf. I've frequently said that good psychology won't overcome bad physics—if you have certain swing flaws, you should seek to get them corrected on the practice tee—but sound thinking can only enhance your performance. A good way of looking at it is this: if you follow the principles and ideas in this book, you'll put yourself in the best possible position—both physically and mentally—to put the best swing you have that day on each shot. That's all you truly owe yourself, regardless of your skill level.

The genesis for this book—and my current work— probably dates to the early 1960s, before I returned to school to earn my doctoral degree in educational psychology. As an assistant basketball coach at tiny Glasgow High School in my native state of Kentucky, I saw firsthand how savvy thinking could help players perform to the best of their abilities. At the time, all teams were privy to the same instructional materials, and the "Xs and Os" didn't differ much among teams. It was evident to me that the coaches who were able to get their teams to focus on a task, and be mentally tough, were the ones who won the most games. Although I returned to graduate school and left coaching, the group of kids that I had coached on the junior varsity squad for two years later won the Kentucky state high school championship. And since Kentucky's was an "open" tournament usually won by the bigger schools from Lexington or Louisville, it was quite an accomplishment for the boys from this small town.

It's generally conceded that the Eastern bloc countries were the first to develop advanced sports psychology techniques with their Olympic teams. The use of techniques stemming from sports psychology research became popular in the United States in the 1960s and came into full flower in the 1970s and 1980s. I began working with golfers on the mental challenges of this sport in 1975, and for a couple of years I didn't charge any of the players for my services—I figured I was learning as much as I was teaching. I don't know if I was the first sports psychologist to work systematically with golfers, but certainly I was among the first. By the 1980s, I was one of a couple of sports psychologists who were specializing in working with elite golfers, and I've been fortunate to be able to work with a number of fine players. They include former PGA and U.S. Open champion Payne Stewart, 1991 PGA Tour money leader Corey Pavin, Ben Crenshaw, Scott Simpson, and Mark O'Meara, along with Dewitt Weaver, Jr., Gene Littler, and Phil Rodgers of the Senior PGA Tour and Donna Andrews of the LPGA.

Equally important for you, the reader, I've also counseled less-skilled golfers—many at golf schools where I've worked—and gotten valuable insight from the men and women on the front lines of golf instruction: the teaching professionals of America, to whom I give educational seminars. I have learned something from every player and teacher with whom I've worked.

The most pleasing thing about my research into golf psychology is that much of it has been corroborated by talking to great athletes in golf and other sports that I have had the chance to know personally, people such as Jack Nicklaus and Michael Jordan. Often, the best athletes have determined by trial and error and their superb instincts the very same principles that sports psychologists have discovered through systematic research techniques. This has been very reassuring for me, since these athletes have tested their principles under pressure and at the highest levels of competition. This book will save you from a lot of hunting and pecking for the answers to the proper mental approach to golf. The time you save can be used to sharpen your physical game on the practice tee.

The principles of sports psychology, whether I'm teaching them to Payne Stewart or to you, don't have to be mystifying or complicated. Some will take more time and consideration to grasp than others, while some will hit you like a bright beam of light on a dark highway. You'll say to yourself, "I knew that" or "That makes sense."

But just like in trying to change the mechanics of your swing to stop slicing, the development of a sound mental approach to golf doesn't come overnight. In fact, one of the first points I try to make to students of all ability levels is that improving the mental side of your game is a journey of peaks and valleys. You don't learn to strike the ball like a tour pro in a day, nor will you be able to learn to think like one that quickly. Unlike some people who are dabbling in golf psychology, I don't believe that you can sit on the clubhouse veranda or in the recliner in your den and simply "think your way" to better golf. It will take time and effort, and different individuals will make the applications in ways unique to their personalities. When I work with golfers, I treat each as an individual; there is no formula for everyone!

I can promise, however, that if you apply yourself to the lessons I'll talk about in these pages, it will be a worthwhile journey. We'll address topics from why golf demands so much mentally, to choosing an instructor, to the all-too-common problem of not being able to take your game from the practice range to the first tee. I'll cover how to develop a sound preshot routine, what to do during those rounds when "the wheels start to come off," and I'll explain how there are two different types of concentration required to play golf well. And at the conclusion of the book, a Golfer's Personality Profile will help you to understand your game better as well as put the lessons of the book to good use in a personalized manner.

The Reason for This Book

So whether you're someone who struggles to break 100 or someone who is disappointed when you don't break par, pull up a chair. Regardless of your skill level, you already have found that golf is a mental game. But what does that really mean? And how can you be a more effective thinker on the course and have more fun in the process? Golf is indeed a mystery, but it's much more solvable than you might think.

Michael Jordan was recently talking about golf on one of his videotapes. He said, "The mind comes into this game so much. It comes into basketball, too, but sometimes your skills can overcome the mind a little bit. But in golf, if your mind's not in it, then you can forget it." This book is about getting your mind on golf.

CHAPTER

THE MIND
AND GOLF

Why do you even try to play golf? No doubt every golfer has tried to answer that question while struggling to finish a round when nothing seemed to be going right. Or maybe it struck you as you were putting in some more tokens in the range-ball machine, in another quest to find "the secret." Perhaps it was in the hotel corridor and you kept getting strange glances as you used the hallway's mirrors to check your position at the top of your backswing. (Don't worry— there was probably a fellow golfer standing there knowing exactly how you felt.)

Golfers are members of a fraternity of millions. We have our own reasons for paying all that money for a club membership or greens fees, or for the privilege of being tutored by an esteemed teaching professional or for the right to hit another bucket of range balls that look like they should have been taken out of circulation when Jack Nicklaus still wore a crew cut.

The game gets its hooks into us, all right. In working with numerous touring professionals, I often have to get their minds off golf before I can get their thoughts focused the right way. One tour player was a particularly tough case in this regard. He seemed never to be able to get his mind off golf. It was his life. He thought about the game morning, noon, and night and was grinding himself into mental and physical exhaustion. I suggested he try a hobby—to find some diversion. I had about given up hope that he would, then one day I got a call from him.

His voice was as excited as I'd ever heard it. "Doc, I see what you meant. I bought some watercolors the other day and I've been painting away." "That's great," I replied. "What have you been painting?" "Golf course landscapes," he said. I was stuck for an answer.

Why do golfers get hooked on the game? What draws people to golf so that they're unable—or at the least unwilling—to let go?

Golf is an endeavor that offers intermittent reinforcement. That is, its rewards don't come with every shot, every hole, or even every round. And psychological research has found that behaviors that are acquired on the basis of intermittent reinforcement are the behaviors most resistant to extinction. Playing the slot machines or smoking cigarettes are other examples. The slots don't pay off after every pull of the lever, of course, and that's what keeps the customers coming back for more. It's the anticipation of "the hit." A cigarette smoker doesn't enjoy every smoke, but somewhere down the line—after a meal, or with a drink—he knows that one will taste very good. The "hit" and the good cigarette are remembered—the losses and the bad cigarettes are forgotten.

Golf is no different. You're rewarded with feelings of pride, accomplishment, and joy when you strike the solid drive or hole the snaking twenty-footer. But not every shot goes your way, so you're constantly looking, and waiting, for the intermittent reinforcement. It's a powerful concept. When he's asked to defend his superdemanding layouts, golf course designer Pete Dye answers that average golfers enjoy the challenge, and if someone shoots 115, he or she will remember the three good shots hit during the round. Tour pros, on the other hand, will shoot 67 and remember the three bad ones that they hit. Perhaps that's the reason why average golfers line up to play Dye's often-treacherous courses, and why the pros mostly carp about them. Dye is following the principle of intermittent reinforcement; he simply tends to make the average golfer wait longer for a reward than some of the other course architects.

For people who have achieved at a high level in their everyday lives, golf can be an addictive sport. High achievers love activities that are difficult to master, and golf is certainly one of those. "You can never own the secret of golf," says former PGA champion Dave Marr. "You just try to borrow it for periods of time." Unlike bowling, golf's only "perfect game" exists in a golfer's dreams. Even after extremely successful rounds, golfers can reflect on what might have been. Al Geiberger and Chip Beck, who hold the PGA Tour scoring record with 59s—Beck's was shot in 1991—still probably left the scoring tent considering the shot that got away.

In other words, golf is always an unfinished task. Ben Hogan, Arnold Palmer, and even Nicklaus have never completed golf. There is always more to learn, more to experience, more challenges to be met. It's interesting that we speak of rounds of golf, since true rounds have no beginnings or ends. This is how avid golfers view it. Evidence that people are drawn to activities such as this dates back to the 1920s and 1930s, to research done by developmental psychologists Maria Ovsiankina and Bluma Zeigarnik. Ovsiankina found that when people were given activities to do and then were interrupted, they consistently returned to these tasks far more often than to activities they were allowed to complete. Zeigarnik discovered that people consistently remembered unfinished activities more than completed ones, almost as if a tension exists in the person to complete things. Since we never complete golf, we are always anxious to return to the course for another round. Our everyday life is an interruption that intrudes on our golf games.

And because golf is such a difficult activity to master, when you're able to achieve a record score, or merely par a hole that you've never been able to par before, the achievement means something. Success in golf also can change from course to course and day to day, depending on weather conditions. As we see from year to year in the U.S. Open, golfers don't have to shoot 25 under par for seventy-two holes in order to win because the championship course conditions are more demanding than at some of the regular tour stops. A pro will recognize that a good round in the Open will differ from other tournaments, and plan his shots accordingly. For you, expectations might change if you move to the back tees from your customary spot on the middle markers. Or bad weather conditions can change real par from 72 to 76.

When you do break 90 for the first time, you can look forward to then breaking 80. After that, 70. If any golfer, of any skill level, is unable to come up with meaningful goals, he's not thinking very hard, or very creatively.

From working with all types of golfers, I constantly see

at how many levels the game can be played, which is another of its lures. I've helped golfers whose main goal was cutting out one disastrous hole so they could finally break 90, and in helping tour golfers fine-tune their talents, I've seen just how well this game can be played.

I've also been around other sports played at their highest levels, but nothing seems to match the electricity of being on the practice tee just before teeing off in the final round of a major golf championship. I remember being with Payne Stewart at Royal Troon in Scotland at the 1989 British Open Championship. Payne and Tom Watson, who were both near the lead, were the last two players to leave the practice tee. The two players weren't far apart on the tee, and I could hear what Watson's longtime mentor, the great Byron Nelson, was saying to his man as they finished up. Interestingly, Mr. Nelson wasn't talking about any high-level supersecrets. At this point he was just trying to reassure his pupil that he was on target and was keeping him in focus. This is very similar to what good football and basketball coaches do in pregame talks.

At that juncture, those two world-class golfers (Watson and Stewart) weren't acquiring any skill; they were merely fine-tuning their games for the round ahead. Golf, however, is made more difficult because it consists of two very separate mental components. The first is skill acquisition; the second is playing the game. The kind of personality that makes it easier for you to succeed at the former often makes it harder for you to excel at the latter. Learning how to hit pure, technically correct 5-iron shots with the proper trajectory, for instance, is a requisite to being a good ball-striker, but playing the game well, as we'll go into in detail later, demands a different approach. The perfectionistic attitude that lets you stay on the practice tee for hours and concentrate on learning how to hit that 5-iron can often get in your way on the course. Likewise, if you live by a "let it happen" philosophy, which can help you as you play the game, it may not be beneficial during practice sessions. You need to be aware of these factors and your own personality in this regard. We shall return to this theme in greater detail later in the book.

To nongolfers, the game can seem silly. We've all heard the snide remarks about how hard can it be to knock a little, dimpled ball—a stationary ball, at that—around until you find a slightly larger hole. Until I took up golf in my early twenties, I didn't think much differently. I had played baseball in high school and college, and having had some success at standing up at the plate and using a bat to hit a ball that was moving toward me at eighty or ninety miles per hour, golf looked like it would be a cinch.

I was wrong, of course, as are many who try to transfer their talents from other sports to golf. There is no teammate to blame for your troubles. There is the fear of looking foolish. Mostly, though, there is the fact that golfers have to initiate all the action. Golfers don't get to react to an opponent's serve or defensive position. Moreover, golfers have to wait considerable periods of time between shots before initiating the action. Golf is a game of starting and stopping, making it hard to find and maintain a rhythm and flow to your game. Proof that this is the aspect that creates such a challenge in golf is that in many other sports, slumps most often occur at positions or activities where the participant is initiating the action, rather than reacting to it. Examples are kicking field goals in football, shooting free throws in basketball, and serving in tennis.

While those are similarities between golf and other sports, let's consider one very visible example where golf is much different: consider the way golfers treat their golf clubs—naming them and otherwise treating them as if they were alive and breathing. The famous Swiss psychologist Jean Piaget theorized that everyone goes through a stage in our early intellectual life called animism. In this stage we bestow magical power to objects. Golfers, even the best of them, seem to stay in this stage for life. Bobby Jones's putter was dubbed "Calamity Jane" by sportswriters, and the club seemed to have human qualities when he used it. Jones himself named his driver "Jeanie Deans" after a heroine in a novel he read while a student at Harvard. Jack Nicklaus won the 1967 U.S. Open with "White Fang," a center-shafted putter that had been painted white.

All golfers have experienced having a club (or a set of clubs) that seems to hold magic. You browse around a golf shop, pick up a driver, and immediately *know* that this is the one club you've been looking for to complete your arsenal. Usually the club works for a while, but then loses its magic. Once again, you start the search for another animistic driver. Very seldom, however, will a PGA Tour player sell or give away a club even after it has lost its mystical powers. He may "loan" it indefinitely to a fellow pro, but he is most unwilling to part with it permanently, because he believes the magic could return if he decides to play with it again someday. Why do clubs seem to lose their magic over time? No one knows for sure, but one theory is that as players continually see a particular club squared up behind their ball, they make mental accommodations to this same sight and develop a stale perception to the ball-club relationship. This sense of stimulus overfamiliarity, or stimulus redundancy, is comparable to a person who has been married for many years and fails to notice small changes in his partner like a new hairstyle or new frames for her glasses.

While I'm convinced the psychology of equipment is a critical factor in the lives of golfers, an event occurring at the 1987 Ryder Cup matches did give me reason for pause. Ben Crenshaw, who had been putting with the same classic blade putter since he was a teenager, broke his putter shaft on the sixth hole of his singles match against Eamonn Darcy of Ireland. What a psychological blow it had to be for a player to lose a putter that he had used and trusted for so long, especially in an important event such as the Ryder Cup. It took Crenshaw a couple of holes to get over the shock of being without "Little Ben," but then he holed his share of putts, including a couple of birdies, by putting with his wedge and 1-iron. He squared the match before losing on the eighteenth hole, proving that in this one instance, good physics could overcome bad psychology.

"Little Ben" returned to Crenshaw's bag, however, except for a period a couple of years later when the putter was heisted from his bag at an airport. But an airport employee, who perhaps had played some golf himself, found out about the theft and saw that the club was returned to Crenshaw. Now, Crenshaw could have had the physical characteristics of his beloved putter replicated in another club. But his feeling for it would not have been the same, and when "Little Ben" was finally back in his hands, it was like he had recovered a long-lost friend.

That's how mental a game golf can be. And as we move along in the book, we'll detail why it is so mentally demanding as well. In chapter 3, you'll find out why a split personality of sorts is necessary for good golf.

CHAPTER SUMMARY

- Be aware of the powerful effect of intermittent reinforcement as it relates to golf.
- Recognize, as the great players have, that golf is an unfinished task. There is always another goal to be met, or improvement to be made. This makes the game unique.
- Understand that golf, perhaps more than any other sport, consists of acquiring different skills and then applying them as you play, and each area poses distinct challenges.

C H A P T E R

WHY GOLF DEMANDS
SO MUCH MENTALLY

You don't have to have a split personality to be a good golfer, but it helps. On each shot, golf demands that a player exhibit two entirely different ways of thinking. One is serious, precise, analytic—the golfer is a do-it-by-the-numbers person. The other is creative, impulsive—a free spirit who lives by intuition.

One is the golfer who takes care to thoroughly consider his options on every shot, carefully going through a pre-shot procedure to put himself in the best possible position to hit the best shot he is capable of striking. The other is the golfer who swings the club—or, more accurately, allows it to be swung without overcontrolling it. Recognizing that you, as one golfer, must exhibit both these mind-sets in order to play golf well is crucial to understanding the mental side of the game. You won't fulfill your potential until you acknowledge and understand this dichotomy of golf.

The demand for two different mind-sets is in line with the makeup of the human brain itself. The left hemisphere processes information in a logical, sequential way; it analyzes. The right hemisphere processes emotions, feelings, and creativity. The two sides combine to control our actions, but most individuals tend to be more strongly influenced by one side or the other. Most people are either more analytic or more intuitive.

Analyzers excel in those areas of golf that involve preshot thinking skills. They prefer tasks that call for precise, correct responses with no ambiguities or uncertainties. They revel in reading greens, checking their posture and grip, following a prescribed preshot routine down to the nth degree, using an intermediate target for checking their line, plumb-bobbing putts, and making careful club selections. Pilots, dentists, surgeons, accountants, and engineers practice professions which require them to be very analytic and precise. They consistently bring these tendencies to the golf course with them.

I once played with a professor who was new to golf. He had seen the pros plumb-bobbing their putts, and he asked me why they did it. I quickly told him that I considered plumb-bobbing, at best, a way to verify a break in the green that the player already had noticed. But the professor was fascinated by the precise logical nature of the procedure. By the seventh tee, he had even begun to plumb-bob his tee shots. But even though the number of his plumb-bob attempts went up, his score did not go down.

The plumb-bobbing professor is an extreme example of the overly analytic golfer. But the good news is that this type of golfer rarely makes a mistake before setting his club in motion. He is very good at half the game. At a certain point, however, golf demands that you quit analyzing and start swinging. Forget about being a surgeon and start being a free spirit. Quit trying to make it happen and start letting it happen. You have to go from voluntary to involuntary control. You have to allow feel and intuition to take over—even if that tendency is not within your normal basic nature.

This can be a lot easier said than done for the analytic person who is prone to perfectionism. His personality, which serves him so well before he hits a shot, now begins to interfere. He wants every part of his swing to be in just the right position and sequence, and he frequently finds himself paralyzed by overanalysis—he tries to connect all the dots in his backswing. In seeking control, he loses the natural feel and rhythm so crucial to good shots. The precise dentist, whom I admire so much when I'm in his office chair, becomes a painfully slow, rigid, rhythmless player on the golf course.

In contrast, intuitive persons are highly attuned to their senses and fond of improvising. Many artists, poets, writers, and dancers fit into this category. They are feeling-oriented, with a good sense of how their bodies are moving through space. They respond to something as a whole rather than to its bits and pieces. And they can have trouble following a precise routine.

Once, at a youth golf camp, I was trying to get the golfers to develop a specific routine to use before every shot. In asking questions of the young golfers, I worked my way to the most laid-back kid in the camp. I asked him whether he'd used a preshot routine before. Amazingly, he told me that he had. Asking him to elaborate on his routine, he said, "It's simple. I do a little bit of this and a little bit of that. And then I rears back and whops it." John Daly won the 1991 PGA Championship with a preshot routine that consisted of his caddie saying "Kill" before each shot.

Intuitive golfers are very good once the club is moving, but they often make mistakes before the swing begins because they don't like to discipline themselves to think through the demands of a particular shot. Rather than use an intermediate target for alignment, they saunter up to the ball and squirm around until they feel comfortable. Then, as my young friend said, they "whops" it. If you're an extremely intuitive golfer, you most likely make errors in club selection, hole strategy, and reading the greens. Since you play largely by feel, however, you usually have a great touch on short shots and a great imagination for trouble shots.

The category of intuitive golfers might include the great creative shotmakers—Seve Ballesteros, Tommy Bolt, Sam Snead, Ben Crenshaw, Lanny Wadkins, and Payne Stewart. You often can easily spot an intuitive golfer off the course. Stewart is a good example. While driving around Scotland with Payne and several other friends the week before the 1991 British Open to play some of that country's wonderful golf courses, I saw how Payne's intuition worked on the road. Our group was armed with every kind of map and highway atlas that we could find, yet Payne maneuvered our rented van through those small Scottish towns without looking at any of the maps. He "felt" his way around, as is his basic nature on the golf course.

The analyzers would likely include Ben Hogan, Cary Middlecoff, Tom Kite, Nick Faldo, Steve Pate, and Bobby Clampett. This type of golfer loves to dissect the swing and understand its every move. He often loves spending lots of time on the practice tee, and he enjoys talking about swing mechanics with fellow golfers and swing instructors. Neither pattern is better than the other; they are just very different ways to play. It's my view that Jack Nicklaus is the best at combining the two ways of thinking—the two personalities, if you will. Moreover, he is able to change his way of thinking in a matter of seconds to allow his swing to happen without overcontrolling it.

To a casual observer watching Nicklaus perform on the golf course, the overriding impression is one of methodical precision. But having seen Nicklaus at work several times in his other profession—golf course architecture—I can attest that a creative side exists within him. While walking a piece of property that soon will be a Nicklaus-designed golf course, he is every bit the artist as he surveys the land, making hand gestures and drawing his impressions on a sketchpad.

Related to personality style is conceptual tempo, the speed at which a person makes decisions. A person may respond quickly (have an impulsive tempo) or slowly (a reflective tempo) in a situation where there is a high response uncertainty—that is, where you're unsure how you'll react. For instance, when you are asked your name, there is a high response certainty—you know what you're going to say and you answer quickly and accurately. On the golf course, however, as in our daily lives, plenty of situations exist where several viable alternatives seem possible. Is it a hard 8-iron to the green or an easy 7-iron? Should I cut the ball in over the bunker or try to run it through the narrow opening at the front of the green? These are high-response-uncertainty situations.

People with an impulsive conceptual tempo tend to make quick decisions and often make mistakes because they don't consider all the variables or all the possible strategies in a given situation. They just grab a club and hit, hoping by chance it will all work out. A friend of mine, for instance, has never figured out how different types of uneven lies affect the flight of his ball, and he continues to hit poor shots from such positions. The person with a reflective conceptual tempo will take time to consider all the important aspects of a situation, and the available strategies, then make his choice. As you might expect, analytical golfers tend to have a very reflective conceptual tempo.

In addition to Nicklaus, Tom Kite and Raymond Floyd are good examples of reflective players. They rarely make an error because of poor thinking. They are not slow players, however. The majority of the information that needs to be processed can be handled as you approach your ball or while your playing companions are hitting their shots.

Too many less-skilled golfers attempt to emulate Nicklaus by standing over their putts long after they have quit actively processing information. They eventually draw a blank mentally—I call it a synaptic shutdown—and frequently their putt "goes off in their hands" and goes nowhere near the hole. While Nicklaus looks to be taking a very long time before he takes the putter back and therefore might be susceptible to synaptic shutdown, he actually has no sense of how long he is taking. Why? Because he is so totally engrossed in processing the variables related to his putt; he is far from standing blank over the ball. Conversely, a fine player such as Lee Trevino, who counts six major championships among his many victories, looks as if he hardly gets set over the ball before he begins his swing. Trevino simply has an impulsive conceptual tempo and he plays within his personality, just as Nicklaus plays within his.

However quickly Trevino plays, he still is paying close attention to the many preshot variables. No player of his caliber can be that good without thinking appropriately about where to aim the ball, the intended flight of the ball, the intended target, club selection, how the lie affects ball flight, and so on. Tour players go through many more variables than the average player because they know so much more about the game. In fact, when an average golfer rightly begins to incorporate a sound preshot routine into his or her game, it feels awkward. It's analogous to an airline pilot with twenty years' experience and one right out of training. Both will accomplish the same thing, and both are detail-oriented when running through a preflight checklist, for example, but the veteran can do things more fluidly, while still doing them sequentially.

The tour player can easily be compared with the veteran pilot. From outside the ropes at a tournament, or watching on television, you look at the pros and see such effortless movements, before and during their swings. They have eliminated the unnecessary movements. (Keep in mind, though, that until the past couple of years and the advent of early-round coverage of pro events on TV, we never saw a tour pro who wasn't on the leaderboard, who wasn't playing very well.) Rest assured that there is a huge difference between a tour pro contending for a title and one who is struggling to make his first thirty-six-hole cut in a month; the latter is most often the type of golfer who comes to seek my help.

When tour pros start playing badly toward the end of the season or at the conclusion of a long run of consecutive events earlier in the year, it's often because they get what they call "brain dead"—that is, they stop paying attention to the dozen or so decisions that a golfer needs to make before he sets the club in motion. The skilled professional knows what the decisions are, but he is too tired or uninterested to make them in a considered and conscious fashion. Most average golfers, on the other hand, don't understand the details of the preshot procedure. The worst offenders, often beginners, don't give themselves a fighting chance for success regardless of their physical ability.

Many golfers make bad decisions during the preswing: posture or grip may be bad or alignment may be off. They just hope that all the negatives cancel out each other, and in the process—or, actually, lack thereof—they've put themselves in a corner before they've begun to swing.

If you're an analytical person with a job that relies on precise decisions and movements, you might very well be good at the analytic side of golf. But you may not be as skilled at the game as you would like. An ear, nose, and throat surgeon whom I know does many microsurgery procedures each month that demand very fine motor control. Yet, as a golfer, he can't understand why he is a poor putter, the aspect of the game that most depends on precise, small movements. The doctor's mentality transfers all right, but his physical skills as a surgeon don't transfer to the putting green.

For analytical and intuitive golfers alike, one of the

biggest mental challenges of the game is that unlike most other sports that require good aiming, golfers don't focus on the target while they swing. Within the dichotomy of a preshot routine and a free-flowing swing, the notion of a target that we're not looking at is always present. The respected golf instructor Bill Strausbaugh once noted that golfers would be better off if they had been born with one eye in the middle of the forehead and the other eye where our left ear is (for right-handed golfers). Strausbaugh was talking about the difficulty that golfers have in looking at one target—the ball—and hitting it to another, the intended landing area.

In most sports our vision starts out on the primary target and we continue to focus on it as we shoot a basket, pass to a wide receiver, or throw a baseball. There are some exceptions, such as tennis and football placekicking, but during most athletic endeavors both of our eyes are focused on the primary target throughout the action. Strausbaugh talks about the mind's eye being on one target (the landing area) and the optic eye on a different target (the ball).

Expanding on Strausbaugh's ideas, I believe that good players focus their attention during a shot in a much different manner than poor players. This difference relates to both the analytic (preswing) and intuitive (actual swing) part of the game. The differences show up in the way golfers approach the three variables that must be given simultaneous attention: (1) the primary target, (2) the ball, and (3) how the body and club are to be moved so the ball goes to the target.

Both good and poor players attend to each of these variables, but they differ significantly in the level of awareness given to each. The good players first become oriented to the primary target, which might be either a fairway landing area or green. They do this by going into broad external focus, their eyes sweeping the target area looking for bunkers, water hazards, out-of-bounds stakes, and the slope of the land. Then, they lock in on a smaller area within that larger framework, which becomes their desired landing area. After that, they choose an intermediate target, or aiming point, which is one to two feet in front of the ball and in line with the actual target. This intermediate point becomes their compass, keeping them oriented to the landing zone.

Good players focus their eyes on the ball sufficiently to allow their hand-eye coordination to work for them throughout their swing. But they aren't so homed in to the ball that they become fixated on it, or ball-bound. They are simply aware that the ball is there. During the swing, the good player does not dwell on the target or the ball—though there is a small bit of perceptual awareness on both—but, instead, on the sense of the swing. That is, how his body is going to feel when it produces the swing that lets the ball go to the target.

This is the intuitive part of golf that the good player does so much better than his less-skilled counterpart. By focusing on this swing sense instead of a checklist of mechanical movements (things such as left arm straight, right elbow tucked in close, left hip turning), the good player is able to produce a sound swing which takes the ball to the intended target.

Poorer players do not apportion their levels of awareness the same way. They tend to be too focused on the ball and too aware of the trouble in the landing area. You can tell when someone has trouble with these levels of awareness by watching him swing at a dandelion or cigar butt, then looking at him swing with a ball teed up. On the dandelion swing, the golfer probably has respectable rhythm, pace, and tempo, enough so to make you think he is swing-sense-focused.

But when the swing is for real, with a ball in front of him, it's a different story. He becomes fixated on the ball and too aware of too many mechanical movements during the swing. The resulting shot is often poorly hit.

In his 1946 book, *On Learning Golf,* the British teaching legend Percy Boomer keenly addressed the appropriate mind-set necessary to a golfer once he's begun his swing. "You must be mindful but not thoughtful as you swing," Boomer wrote. "You must not think or reflect; you must feel what you have to do. Our golfing self should be concerned with . . . the movements necessary to produce a good shot. These movements are controlled by remembered feel and the only concentrating we must do is guarding this 'remembered feel' from interference."

The problem with golf is that you must switch from the analytic nature of a rocket scientist to Boomer's "remembered feel" in a matter of a few seconds on each shot. There is no bigger challenge in the game.

CHAPTER SUMMARY

• Golf calls for you to be both analytical and intuitive in order to play well.

- Understand your personality style and how it relates to the two distinct ways of processing information necessary in golf.
- The speed at which you make decisions also affects your game. Determine if you are impulsive or reflective on the course.
- In most sports, an athlete's eyes are focused on the primary target throughout the action. Because golf is different, you need to be concerned with where your attention is focused, and at what level, during a shot.

C H A P T E R

LEARNING AND RELEARNING
HOW TO PLAY

Although there have been thousands of magazine articles, books, and videos produced to show people how to play golf, there has been considerably less attention paid to the understanding of that learning process. In other words, many people don't know "how to learn," or how to learn about golf. And from the mental standpoint of the game, this is a big omission, because whether you're learning golf for the first time or trying to refine your swing for the fortieth time, whether your handicap is 4 or 24, you no doubt can use some help while getting help.

Should someone try to tell you that learning golf is a snap, he's wrong. The very reasons that have been mentioned previously as drawing people to golf—indeed, getting them hooked on the game—are the same reasons why it's such a difficult sport to grasp. And no matter what article you read, book you buy, tape you watch, or instructor you visit, you can't escape the fundamental truth that golf is not an easy game. Fortunately, however, strategies exist to make the learning—or relearning—of golf somewhat easier. If you consider these when you set out to educate yourself, you'll give yourself your best chance at being the best player you can be. A little thinking at the outset can save a lot of strokes down the road.

DON'T GO IT ALONE

Perhaps more than athletes in any other sport, many golfers take an odd bit of pride in saying that they've never had a golf lesson. Maybe it's part of the self-made, pull-yourself-up-by-the-bootstraps lore of our country. Maybe the elemental nature of the objective of golf— putting a small ball into a slightly larger hole in the fewest number of strokes—has something to do with it as well.

As difficult as golf is to learn generally, it is much tougher to teach yourself how to play. Although skilled self-made golfers have made their mark in the game's history, they are rare. Jack Nicklaus had Jack Grout. Arnold Palmer had his father, Deacon. Tom Kite and Ben Crenshaw had Harvey Penick. Even Ben Hogan and Sam Snead, two legends who are widely viewed to have been self-taught golfers, took advice from others. If the greats do it, you certainly should.

If you don't, you're simply putting yourself behind the eight ball before you've begun. Too many movements in the golf swing are contrary to what feels natural, especially at first. In fact, what does feel natural is probably wrong. I've seen world-class athletes such as pro football and basketball players—even an athlete as skilled as Michael Jordan—try to teach themselves how to play golf, and most of the things that they do naturally to provide power or leverage in their given sport don't work in golf. The instructional book by Hall of Famer Julius Boros may have had the best title of all: *Swing Easy, Hit Hard.* Golf, in fact, can seem to be a game full of contradictions such as that one. If you don't have someone to show you the way, those contradictory messages will be all the harder to understand.

Another reason to start out with sound instruction is what I call the primacy effect. That is, there is a tendency for the first-learned behavior to resurface under pressure, regardless of how much has been learned since. Say a person is a German native who later learned English and used this second language in everyday life. If that person is thrown into a stressful situation, he very well may spontaneously start speaking German. In golf, that's why it's so important to learn appropriately from the beginning, so that a good swing won't be layered over a bad swing which can pop out at the wrong time. This is particularly true with golfers who learn bad habits as juniors; those habits can be doubly hard to break years later, especially if the junior golfer played a lot and deeply ingrained poor technique into his game.

A final reason to seek help when taking up golf is the fear factor. Golf can be full of fear—of failure and of success—but for the beginner it is almost always the former. He can be afraid of looking stupid in front of his friends, of appearing like an uncoordinated klutz if he whiffs the ball. If you set out in golf alone, those fears are magnified, and you have less chance of overcoming them and succeeding at the game.

Once you decide to seek some help with your game, do the right thing and hook up with a qualified teaching professional. Pros earn those PGA of America certificates on their pro shop walls for a reason: they've proven they can teach. Instruction will cost you money in any case, and you're much better off investing in a qualified instructor.

THE PROPER APPROACH TO INSTRUCTION

Among my educational activities over the past several years have been sessions with PGA teaching professionals to try to help them become better instructors. In spending hour after hour on practice tees watching the professionals teach, I have reaped an additional benefit: I've gotten to see firsthand how the students learn. Unfortunately, most pupils make it harder on themselves than it has to be. The good part about this is that you can benefit from their mistakes.

Do you see yourself in one of the following groups of students?

The Know-It-Alls. In contrast to the beginning golfer who may not know much about the game, these pupils have read so many instructional books and viewed so many videos that they get on the practice tee with their instructor and forget who is supposed to be the teacher. In trying to impress the instructor with how much they think they know about their swing and the game in general, they waste the time and energy of themselves and their instructor.

The Professional Students. These students, often wealthy enough to travel around the country visiting the well-known golf schools and taking individual lessons from the marquee instructors, take more delight out of telling folks back at their home club where they've been and who has been teaching them than they do in learning golf. Concerned more about the status of the instructor than the substance of their instruction, these pupils end up getting less out of the lessons than if they had sought help closer to home with a dedicated teacher on a consistent basis.

The Doubting Thomases. For this bunch of students, no instruction is good enough, no matter who the instructor is. Regardless of what the teacher suggests, these cynics question its validity and often are unable to realize when some very good instruction is presented. They would be much better off approaching their lessons with a more open mind.

To help you get the most out of your instruction, consider the following six suggestions. They are valid whether you are new to golf or an experienced player and hold true regardless of your handicap.

1. Agree on instructional objectives with your pro. This sounds simple enough, but many teaching pros have told me this is their number-one problem. If you're just looking for some quick fixes—Band-Aid Lessons, as the pros call them—this is much different than committing to a series of lessons in which the pro helps you revamp your whole swing or approach to the game. Sometimes, if you're visiting a resort, for instance, you may only have time for a quick lesson. Many resort-based teachers specialize in these kinds of lessons, but just keep in mind that while you may be getting a Band-Aid, your swing really might need major surgery.

In setting up your instructional objectives with your teacher, clear communication is vital. Your goals should be in line with your athletic ability, your golf skill level, your physical strength and flexibility, and the amount of time that you can realistically expect to spend working on your game. Be frank with your pro about what you want from his help, but remember that he is the expert. Many golfers crave more distance off the tee, but if you're a golfer with minimal ability and strength, you'll probably be better off taking your teacher's advice to work on your short-game skills instead—if your objectives include lower scores.

2. Find the right teacher for you. Just like in other areas of life, some teachers simply won't click with you, while others will seem like an old friend from the very first meeting. You will increase your chances of actually learning things if you match your learning style with a comfortable match in teaching style. Consider how you learn. If you're new to golf, think back on how you assimilated information in school, or in other sports. Do you like detailed instruction, or are you more suited to seeing the big picture? Do you learn best from words or images? From watching others? From trying things yourself? Are you easily frustrated? Are you thin-skinned and sensitive to criticism? Your answers to these questions will help guide you in your choice of instructor and instructional styles.

3. Get involved in the process. While you don't want to be one of the know-it-alls or doubters mentioned earlier, you do need to ask intelligent questions if you aren't sure what your pro is trying to tell you. Rephrase his advice in your own words, if that seems to help you understand the point. Try to do what the instructor asks; it doesn't help at all to simply say, "I can't do that." By trying to do it, you may be helping you and your teacher figure out where to go next in your lesson.

4. Be honest, and don't let your ego block your education. Far too often, I've seen golfers with handicaps of 15 and above declare to their teacher that they can carry their tee shots 200 yards or more and that they consistently reach twelve greens per round in regulation. These golfers are either bad at self-assessment or they have an ego problem. If your instructor is a good one, he will question you about your game before he begins to work with you. If you're honest with him, it assists him as a teacher and you as a pupil.

5. Comply with the teacher's orders. Like a patient who has been urged by a doctor to take a prescription or do certain exercises, golf students need to comply with their instructor's recommendations. Unfortunately, golfers are often noncompliers, refusing to do as the instructor asks or following only part of what he suggests. Sticking with new advice from an instructor can be hard to do, as evidenced by the many golfers who spend quite a bit of money on good instruction but then revert to their old ways upon their first trip to the course and a two-dollar nassau with their buddies. It can be tough to do, but you must fight the urge to abandon the new for the familiar when the new way doesn't seem to be quickly working for you. Remember that you often have to regress in order to progress. Many golfers forget this important fact.

6. Be patient. Learning golf, as in developing any psychomotor skill, includes the phenomenon of plateauing. In learning a skill, periods of relatively rapid learning are followed by periods when it is difficult to ascertain any

overt progress. These times of leveling off are called plateaus. It is during these learning plateaus that you need to
be patient and avoid blaming yourself or your instructor. If
you're on the right track with your learning, the plateau
will pass, and firm improvement will occur in time.

TRANSFERRING YOUR TALENTS

While golf poses many challenges distinct from other
sports, some skills used in other sports do transfer to the
game. And since most of us have played other sports at
some point in our lives before we take up golf, this can
work to our advantage. Did you know, for instance, that
both Jack Nicklaus and Ben Crenshaw were pretty good
high school basketball players—Nicklaus for the Upper
Arlington (Ohio) Golden Bears and Crenshaw for the Austin (Texas) Maroons—before giving up basketball to concentrate on golf?

In the past few years, no athlete has gotten more attention for his foray into golf than Michael Jordan of the
Chicago Bulls. Since he went to college where I teach, at
the University of North Carolina at Chapel Hill, I was
around him when he took up golf for the first time in the
mid-1980s, and I vividly recall driving down with Jordan
to Pinehurst, North Carolina, to play thirty-six holes with
him one day at two of the famed resort's courses, Number
2 and Number 6.

It was Jordan's first venture onto championship golf
courses, and being new to the game, he really struggled
over the first eighteen holes. But he didn't get disgusted

with himself or try so hard that he couldn't make any good swings. He simply stuck to his game plan, kept a positive attitude, and by the final nine holes was playing some very solid golf. If Jordan does take up the game systematically after his basketball days are over, it's this kind of attitude—nurtured and defined on the basketball court— that will go a long way toward his achieving his goals in golf.

While you or I don't have Jordan's fantastic athletic skills, we can take what we've learned on other playing fields to the golf course with more success than you might think. From my experience with athletes in other sports, four characteristics seem to transfer consistently from other sports to golf, and vice versa. If you've participated in other sports, you should be able to relate to these traits.

1. Pinpoint concentration for sustained periods. The four hours or so it takes to play a competitive round of golf makes it very difficult to call on intense concentration all the time. You need to learn how to come in and out of concentration. Focusing and refocusing is an important skill. Athletes who have learned how to do this in other sports are at a big advantage when they take up golf.

2. Decision making under pressure. Successful athletes in all sports have to come to grips with this obstacle, but golf especially demands it during stressful competitive moments. Golfers make hundreds of decisions every eighteen holes.

3. The competitive desire to succeed. This trait can be accompanied by the ability not to give up until the round is over and a sense of self-confidence that allows the player to maintain a strong belief that he will beat his opponent. He doesn't worry about what his foe is doing, and this certainly applies to golf, which doesn't permit you to defend against your competition.

4. Don't play what you don't practice. Although this maxim frequently is overlooked by golfers, if you've played other sports you should be more resistant to it than someone who hasn't. Think about your high school football days, if that's what you participated in. You had a coach, and your team wouldn't think of running plays during the games on Friday nights that you hadn't practiced during the week. If you apply this to your golf game, you'll be way ahead of many golfers who often try shots—difficult shots—on the course that they've never even tried in practice.

AVOIDING THE OVEROBSERVING TRAP

An old Danish proverb says that "He who builds according to every man's advice will have a crooked house." Turned into a modern-day golfing proverb it might read, "He who builds a golf swing according to every man's advice will hit many crooked shots."

All the instruction-taking advice talked about earlier in this chapter is for naught if you fall into the all-too-common trap of listening to too many voices, or reading too many words about the golf swing. Though this phenomenon may be as old as the game itself, the proliferation, and acceptance of, golf instruction during the past twenty years has increased the chances that you are building yourself a crooked house or crooked swing.

There is not one golf swing for everybody, but I do

believe there is a golf swing that fits each of us as individuals. This swing is right for you because it takes into account your body type, flexibility, age, available practice time, inherent athletic ability, and your commitment to the game—the very things that you should discuss with your instructor, as pointed out earlier.

Many golfers fail to find "their swing," however, because they are too busy looking around. They observe and listen too much. The tendency to compare ourselves against the swings of others occurs at all playing levels, from the golfers in the nine-hole summer twilight league to the professional tours—often especially on the pro tours.

Out on the tours, players talk about becoming "Hoganized," a reference to the preoccupation with other players' mechanical technique and applying it to one's own swing. It's a reference to Ben Hogan, the golfer known for his concern with the technical aspects of hitting a golf ball. Often the players becoming Hoganized are also afflicted by "rabbit ears," the propensity to listen too much to too many conflicting pieces of information. The rabbit ears problem usually strikes young players new to the tour, but it can affect veterans as well, particularly now as older players, perhaps off the regular tour for a while, prepare to go out on the Senior PGA Tour once they turn fifty years old.

Getting players away from observing and listening too much is something I often do when tour players come to me for help. What I try to tell them is that to become a good player, you don't have to know *the golf swing*, you have to know *your golf swing*. Everybody's swing on tour is a little different, but the successful players are the ones who may not know *the* swing, but they surely know their own. They are much better off that way. When golfers get caught up in trying to understand everything about *the golf swing*, they are setting themselves up for trouble.

When tour golfers come seeking my help, they often ask, "Doc, can you just get me back to playing like I did when I was a kid?" What they mean is less mechanically oriented, with fewer variables in their swing. They long for the simpler, more natural swing of their youth. And they are correct in wanting to search for it.

Gary Hallberg, the gifted former four-time All-American at Wake Forest, got caught up in knowing the golf swing instead of his swing, and he now acknowledges that this has hurt his career on tour. In working over the past couple of years to recapture his swing—the one that made him such a wonderful golfer in his early twenties—Hallberg has realized that his responsibility is to understand how his action works instead of trying to make a life of understanding how the swing works. He realizes that he is better off leaving that to swing instructors who make it their life's work to figure out the swing.

One of the saddest cases of a talented player suffering from overanalysis and observation is that of the late Ralph Guldahl, who won consecutive U.S. Open championships in 1937–38 and the Masters in 1939. At the height of his career, Guldahl was contracted to write a golf instructional book. He took to the task seriously, holing up in a room for weeks at a time, swinging in front of a mirror, dissecting his swing as a model for the instruction he would write. Guldahl got the book done, but in writing it he became so overly analytic in regard to his swing that he never was able to achieve the greatness of earlier in his career.

While you're not going to be asked to write an instructional book, you can fall victim to overanalysis and over-observation in many ways. I'm certainly not deriding instructional articles in golf publications—I write them myself on the mental side of the game—but you need to be selective in what you read and how you allow an article to influence your game. While every instructional article probably connects with someone who reads it, not every article is for everyone. A friend of mine is a devoted reader of the monthly golf publications, and if he's just received his magazines, he plays a shaky first few holes because he's intent on trying every piece of instruction that he's just read.

The smart way to approach instructional articles, books, or videotapes is to understand your swing and have an educated idea of what advice might be relevant for you. Some methods of instruction are geared to the strength, flexibility, and practice time that tour players and advanced amateurs have. If you don't have those attributes, approach the "tour pro tells how" articles with some trepidation. Try them, if your curiosity is that great, but try them knowing that the instruction probably won't fit you.

Articles featuring John Daly's long swing appeared shortly after his surprise victory in the 1991 PGA Championship. While I thought the photographs were fun to look at, Daly's swing has so many moving parts and requires such hand-eye coordination that you would probably be wasting your time if you decided to go out to the practice range and turn your swing into Daly's. The best thing you can glean from Daly is that his swing is his own, and he understands it.

While there is no sure way to avoid observing too much, there are a couple of things you can do to alleviate the tendency. First, learn to observe selectively. Listen to a few people who know the mechanics of the swing and who also are familiar with your swing. Learn enough about your swing so that you can filter out information from others that might harm, rather than help, your game. If you don't have a clear understanding of your game, you'll have a poorer chance of figuring out what will enhance it.

HAVE YOU GOT A SECRET?

Along the road of learning about golf, you will find yourself one day saying, "I've got the secret now." Think about how often you've said those words after taking a lesson or reading or viewing some instructional material. It can seem that the search for the secret is what binds golfers together, as everyone goes out looking to solve the big riddle with one change, one tip, one last alteration to make things just right. What about these secrets? Is there such a thing? Should you try to find the secret to your swing?

I think golfers should indeed search for the secret while recognizing that the secret differs from golfer to golfer and changes over time, even for the same golfer. I define a secret as a key or cue that brings together the parts of your game in the right way. The real secret is to identify

LEARNING AND RELEARNING HOW TO PLAY

what the key is for you at a given point in time. You'll need to reidentify what will help you the most as your game changes. Thinking about a full extension on the backswing may have been the key at some point, but now it might be thinking about the right hip turn. Down the road, it might be something entirely different. This is even true for the best players on the pro tours.

What causes a swing tip to work great for one round, or for that matter, for one hole, then to go away and leave you swinging as poorly as ever? This is one of the mysteries of the game. It may be because of fatigue, boredom, lack of opportunity to practice or play, or inattention to grip, setup, or posture. Or you simply may be overdoing the secret that worked in the first place.

Johann Herbart, a nineteenth-century German philosopher, never played golf but he may have had a possible explanation for the short life of secrets. Herbart explained that people bring to each situation in life an "apperceptive mass"—an accumulation of all our past experiences. This apperceptive mass is full of our old and new ideas, and changes as we learn new things. As our apperceptive mass changes, we see things differently. Take the case of rereading a novel or textbook. You might come across passages or paragraphs that you highlighted or underlined the first time you read the book. Upon rereading it, you may be puzzled why you chose those certain passages to highlight and why you didn't emphasize others. According to Herbart's theory, your apperceptive mass has changed between the first and second times you read the book.

In golf, our apperceptive mass changes from day to

day, for golfers of all skill levels. Some days, the keys to a good round won't lie on the mechanical swing side, but on the mental side. Other days, for the same player, it might be a very mechanical swing key. The secret may be in the setup position, for instance.

The best way to manage your golfing secrets is to recognize that your apperceptive mass changes from day to day and to know where to search for your secrets. The simplest and best way is to jot down in a notebook your given thoughts on a day when your swing worked well. This can be your guide to refer to and may save you a lot of frustration, since there is so much to learn that you end up forgetting a lot of it and it ends up seeming new again, which in turn can make it more difficult to grasp.

To give yourself a better chance of finding the secret, come up with several keys for the mental side, the setup, and the swing. Write them down, and when you set out to find them again, you'll at least know where to turn. You will have put yet a little more order in your search to learn golf, a search that will continue as long you play the game.

CHAPTER SUMMARY

- Don't kid yourself that golf is an easy game to learn. Seek help from a qualified instructor.
- Learn proper skills at the outset, because your first learned behavior has a tendency to resurface in pressure situations.

- Consider your learning style when you pick an instructor.

- If you've played other sports, think of ways to transfer your talents to golf.

- Observe selectively. Listening to too many voices can hinder the learning process.

C H A P T E R

FROM THE PRACTICE TEE
TO THE FIRST TEE

For many golfers, the idea of practice means going to the driving range and whacking away at as many of the striped balls as quickly as possible—the "driver as machine-gun" approach. Before you know it, the bucket of balls that you pounded out is already being scooped up by the fellow in the enclosed tractor. You may have worked up a sweat and massaged your ego by trying to send a few balls out to the yardage signs at the far end of the range, but you've probably done very little to help your game.

Very few golfers understand what is involved in a smart preround warm-up session, and how much such a session would help their games. As a result, they either rush to the first tee after an improper warm-up, or without one at all, and they pay the price by needlessly beginning the round with higher-than-necessary scores on the first several holes. And if you've played much golf at all, you know how a lousy start can sour even the brightest of sunny spring days. Still another group of golfers falls victim to what's known in baseball as "White Line Fever." That is, they hit good shots on the practice tee but can't transfer their ability once they cross the white line from practice tee to the course.

The worst thing about *poor* practice habits is how unnecessary they truly are. With some smart thinking, you can give yourself the best chance to develop your ability during practice sessions, and to play up to your potential by going through a fundamentally sound preround warmup. You don't have to be a low-handicap golfer to accomplish either of those goals; you just have to want to improve your golf game.

Along those lines, three thoughts about golf practice spring to mind. First, although the proprietor may call it a driving range, you should get in the habit of referring to it as a practice range, practice tee, or practice area. This in itself should help quell the connotation of a range as a place simply to see how far you can hit the ball. Second, rethink the phrase "Practice makes perfect." A more accurate version for golfers, I believe, is "Perfect practice makes relatively perfect." Third, take stock of this slogan, which is plastered on countless football and basketball locker-room walls: "Many people have the will to win, but not many people have the will to prepare to win." With these thoughts in mind, let's see what smart practice is all about and examine how to transfer your skills from the practice tee to the first tee as efficiently as possible.

It's important to understand that practicing between rounds and warming up before you play are entirely different situations, and should be treated accordingly. A between-round practice session is the time to work on swing changes or dwell on the mechanics of your swing. A preround warm-up is the time to loosen up, to determine any swing or mental-side keys for the day and to generally focus your thoughts for the round ahead of you.

Just take a look at the practice tee the next time you visit a tour event. Before their rounds, when they're warming up, the pros have a much different purpose in mind than late in the afternoon when they've completed play and go back to the practice area. Before teeing off, they're more solitary figures, calm and focused on their round. It's during the between-round practice sessions later in the day that you'll see the pros hitting more balls, talking more with their fellow competitors, and getting more help from their swing instructors. Instituting change in their game is left to these times, not to the preround warm-up.

The best coaches in all sports try their best to simulate game conditions during practice sessions. When getting their teams to hone certain skills that they might be called upon to execute during the final seconds of a game, basketball coaches will have a game clock running during the practice session. If they know their team is going to be on the road playing in a noisy stadium, football coaches have been known to set up loudspeakers blaring crowd noise at practice so their team will become acclimated to the hostile conditions before actually encountering them when the game is on the line.

Fortunately, in golf you don't need time clocks or loudspeakers in order to simulate gamelike conditions; you just need to practice intelligently. While keeping in mind that there are times when you need to concentrate solely on swing mechanics, most practice sessions should be structured so that you are simulating course conditions on the practice tee. Better yet, if you have a chance to do so, utilize a golf course to practice, keeping in mind not to inconvenience the other players or unnecessarily damage the course. Don't forget about practicing your putting, chipping, or sand shots, and remember that the *wrong* kind of practice, such as mindless driver-bashing, is about the worst thing you can do for your game—worse than no practice at all.

Perhaps the most neglected aspect of practice for many amateurs is finding a target and hitting toward it. Among tour players, being properly aligned is at the top of their priorities; they know that improper alignment can lead to a host of other problems. That's why they use clubs or pointer boards laid on the ground to double-check their alignment, and they frequently ask fellow players to confirm that they're lined up where they think they are. Without this help, no golfer can tell when he's lined up properly and when he's not. You should follow the pros' lead and check alignment as they do.

You should never hit balls without having a target, and no matter what your practice area looks like, there is something on it for you to use as a target. While the trend among practice-range builders these days is to construct realistic greens on the range as targets, you can hit to other targets just as effectively. Whether it's a yardage sign, a patch of discolored grass, an old tractor, a distant water tower, or a lone tree, pick something out and use it as your target. One practice range in New York City uses large metal turtles as yardage signs. They also can make a worthwhile, if unusual, target—if you take the effort to use them.

Tour pro Paul Azinger, one of the best at hitting low, boring shots, has recalled that he honed his ability while growing up by taking aim on the ball picker-upper as it moved across the range collecting balls. Targets not only help your aim and alignment but also help keep your concentration focused during longer practice sessions.

Use your targets to help you "play" holes on the range. During a practice session, you can simulate an entire round at your course by hitting tee shots and then imagining what kind of second shot you would be left with. If your "tee shot" goes way left "into the woods," try the kind of low, hooking recovery shot you would be faced with if you were on a real hole. This type of practice takes effort and concentration but is also enjoyable. If you're practicing with a friend, you both can "play."

Another way to practice with a friend is to try to call shots. You may choose a target 150 yards away, select a 6-iron, and say that you're going to hit a low fade to the target. Your friend has to hit a similar shot, and whoever hits closest to the target gets to call the next shot. This drill can help you to imagine different kinds of shots and be able to use them on the course. This type of practice helps you learn to play golf rather than just be a ballstriker who can't score.

If you're warming up before a round, you can also "play" on the range by simulating the first hole, the first three holes, or a particular hole that gives you trouble. By tackling the trouble on the practice tee, the real trouble on the course may seem less of a problem for you.

While working with Payne Stewart at the 1991 U.S. Open, I saw a good example of this. As Payne warmed up for the fourth round at Hazeltine National Golf Club, he took the time to go over to a nearby practice bunker and hit several middle iron shots out of it before he went to play the final round. He knew that the course featured several fairway bunkers that came into play, and he wanted to be prepared to play from them. A few hours later, with the championship on the line, Payne found himself in a fairway bunker on the seventy-second hole. He struck a good shot to the edge of the green, made par, and got into the playoff with Scott Simpson, which he won the following day.

Practicing shots that they may encounter on the course is a hallmark of the best golfers. Several years ago I ran into Tom Kite in Austin, Texas, the week before the Masters tournament. He was laying down several large bath towels at different distances as he began to practice his wedge play. I asked him what he was doing, and he said the towels were set out at the different distances he expected to encounter for his third shots at Augusta National's four par-5 holes. Since he knew he would not be able to reach many of the par-5s in two shots, he was working hard on his third-shot approaches. This thorough preparation is one reason Kite has enjoyed so many top-ten finishes at the Masters despite not being an especially long hitter.

As a young man, Gary Player sought to prepare himself for any situation he might ever find on the course. This even included practicing explosion shots from various lies in water hazards. By figuring out how the depth of the water and nature of the soil underneath would affect a shot, Player believed that he would give himself the best chance of succeeding should he need to recover from the water's edge during play.

While you may not want to go to Player's extremes, you can—and should—give yourself a variety of situations during practice. In working on sand shots, don't limit yourself to explosion shots from good lies; practice those from buried and sidehill lies as well. On the practice tee, hit shots from less-than-perfect lies. Drop several balls into divot holes and figure out what changes you need to make in your swing in order to hit acceptable shots from the poor lies.

If you're fortunate enough to be able to find some practice time on the course, try this "two balls/worst ball" drill. Payne Stewart and I have used this one during practice rounds. The first player hits two balls off the tee, and his opponent chooses the worst one for him to play for his second shot. The first player then hits two more shots from that spot, with the opponent continuing to choose the worst ball through the putting green, and the player has to sink two putts from a given position or the opponent will choose the one that misses. This drill—a mind game, in fact—reinforces the importance of consistency in golf. No matter how good your first tee shot is, you must duplicate it in order to make it count. If you make a twenty-footer for birdie, you have to make it again. This is a great workout for players of disparate abilities; the more skilled of the two can play worst-ball with the other playing normally. Even tour players have a tough time shooting close to par playing worst-ball. If you try it, don't be shocked when your score is way above your usual number.

For most of us, the transition from everyday life to a round of golf is a very real switch from a hectic, frantic pace to something that's supposed to be a leisurely, enjoyable way to unwind. How often have you left home too late to arrive at the golf course more than a couple of minutes before your starting time? You get to the first tee with your partners having already hit. A couple of quick practice swings and you've topped your opening drive about one hundred yards. Not until the fourth hole are you catching your breath and feeling any rhythm; by then, your score may be too far gone to rescue.

What you needed was a "decompression routine," a specific set of steps to help ease the switch from everyday life to setting foot on the first tee. These four suggestions may help you make the transition, but remember that you might need to experiment with the routine to make it appropriate for your game and personality.

1. Use a relaxation technique off the course. By learning and practicing one of these techniques, which can be acquired through courses with accredited teachers or developed through the use of audiotapes or books, you will learn the important difference between *allowing* yourself to relax and *making* yourself relax. The important point to remember is that each person will develop a unique manner of relaxation. Regardless of the relaxation technique that you choose, practice it regularly off the course before trying it on the first tee.

2. Listen to some soothing music on the way to the course. By listening to smooth, mellow music—you pick the songs—you're provided with two necessary components for your decompression routine: relaxation and rhythm. Hearing the music during your drive to the course can help you begin to unwind from the pressures of everyday life and sense the rhythmic tempo that a good golf swing needs. Music also can stimulate the intuitive portion of your brain, easing the transition to golf if you are coming to the game from an analytical job.

3. Before you get to the first tee, rehearse swing images you want to use during the round. This is a step that most golfers know will help them, but preround distractions often keep them from doing it. Try hard to set aside some time away from making your bets and socializing to mentally review your most positive and effective swing thoughts. These thoughts may be ones from your last round, or from some other time when you played particularly well. This approach allows you to walk to the first tee with more confidence, reminding yourself of past successes.

4. Isolate yourself, close your eyes, and make a series of long, lazy swings. This is another way to make the switch from hurried everyday life to the course, and allows you to integrate positive images from step 3 into your neuromuscular system. Move away from your playing partners and the hubbub of the starter's shack so that you can concentrate fully on how you are feeling on this particular day. Close your eyes. Some golfers get an increased sense of body feel by adding a warm-up weight to their clubhead. In addition to sensing your feel for the day, you'll also enjoy the additional physical benefit of loosened muscles, which should increase your chances of making a full, completed backswing.

Despite efforts to decompress from everyday life, first-tee jitters still affect many golfers. You might be in the fifth flight of the club championship, but as you stroke the last few practice putts before heading to the first tee, your mind is racing as if it were the U.S. Open. Your mouth is dry, and bad thoughts keep popping into your head.

Competitive golf can take many forms, and for many golfers, the switch from casual to competitive play brings about a strong case of nerves. You shouldn't feel strange, or alone, if this happens to you. Some of golf's best players, such as Bobby Jones and Byron Nelson, experienced strong physiological symptoms of nervousness before they played. Yet these champions learned how to manage their first-tee jitters.

In fact, these golfers would have had more of a problem if they had not experienced these symptoms. Everyone—golfers, baseball players, tennis players, actors, singers—tends to become energized before big events. Tommy Bolt is reported to have said that it's not bad to have butterflies in your stomach, but important that the butterflies are flying in formation.

Research on arousal levels (that's what psychologists call the psychological and physical response to perceived stress) indicates that the relationship between performance and arousal occurs in an inverted-U configuration. This means that up to a point the more highly aroused you are, the better the performance. But after this relationship peaks, any greater arousal level has a negative effect on performance. The peak point varies from person to person. One golfer may need to be almost jittery in order to perform at his best. Another may need to be calmer. You need to discover your arousal level—looking at how you react to everyday crises may help—and find out how it affects your play.

Reading your physiological reactions to stress is also important, because they reflect your internal stress level. High-stress physiological indications include sweaty palms, jiggling feet, rapid and shallow breaths, a rapid pulse, and, surprisingly, yawning. By yawning, you release the tension from constricted muscles around the esophagus. By monitoring your body's reactions to stress, you can be aware of when you are feeling the most stress. If you notice that you're breathing rapidly, you can consciously take some deep, cleansing breaths to help reduce your tension.

If the first tee shot of the day continues to give you problems, keep in mind that your first objective should be to get the ball in play, even if you give up some distance. I call this shot that you can call on to put the ball safely in the fairway a "play" shot. In working with young pros who have failed several times to earn their tour qualifying cards, I've found that helping them develop such a play shot for stressful conditions has been the most important ingredient for later success. This shot is like your second serve in tennis—it doesn't ace anyone, but it puts the ball in play.

Most of these players tend to develop a cut shot as their play shot because it's easier to control when they're physically and emotionally uptight. Some choose to use a 3-wood, some choke down on their driver. Others take a full grip and swing with their driver. Aesthetics aren't important on a play shot. The key is to develop a shot that you can trust under pressure. The only aspect of a play shot that need look pretty is the sight of the ball sitting up nicely in the middle of the first fairway.

For club golfers, a competition also can mean a move away from the familiar. Players who normally hit ten to fifteen warm-up shots find themselves with a bucket of one hundred balls greeting them at the member-guest tournament, and they feel compelled to hit them all. Or they decide to look snazzy and bring out a new pair of shoes and a new glove for the tournament, and as a result they feel different over the ball. You're better off doing and using the familiar.

Related to taking your game from the practice tee to the course are the expectations that you carry with you. Expectations affect many different types of behavior in life, and golf is no exception. Some golfers, for instance, behave differently when they have their favorite 7-iron in hand than when they must hit a shot with a despised 2-iron. While the 7-iron evokes good memories and positive expectations, the 2-iron can be a reminder of poor shots and can create negative expectations.

The 2-iron, because of its decreased loft and longer shaft, indeed may be harder to hit with than the 7-iron, but the element of expectation adds to the dilemma. Many golfers seem to practice more with a club with which they expect to hit well—therefore building in the positive expectations—but avoid those clubs for which they have low expectations. This amplifies their negative expectations for these clubs, and when they're forced to use them on the course, the golfers usually confirm the negative expectations. Thus, a vicious circle, or self-fulfilling prophecy, develops: negative expectations lead to inappropriate behavior, which causes a negative outcome that confirms the negative expectation.

On the other hand, positive expectations can act in the same way with the opposite result. If you believe that you're a good putter, or could be, you'll find the time to practice your putting and in time fulfill your expectations. From a psychological standpoint, expectations relate to performance as indicated in the following model:

1. You develop specific expectations regarding particular parts of your game.
1a. These expectations affect your self-concept, motivation, and level of aspiration.
2. Changes in self-concept, motivation level, and level of aspiration affect—positively or negatively—your behavior.
2a. These behavioral changes affect outcomes—positive and negative—observed on the course.
2b. Observed outcomes—success or failure—confirm your expectations. A self-fulfilling prophecy is created.

Our expectations determine whether we judge a particular shot as a success or failure. Expectations that are either too great or too small can cause trouble. I worked with one tour player who won an event early one year. His expectations soared, and he felt it wasn't a matter of *if* he would win another event that year, but *how many* he would win. His expectations of what was an acceptable shot became outlandishly high, and he never was able to accept it when he hit anything less than a perfect shot. As a result, he played miserably for the remainder of the year.

Conversely, I counseled another player whose swing instructor believed he had as good a swing as anyone on tour. Despite this, the player had unusually low expectations and couldn't envision himself as an equal to the winners on tour. But by increasing his expectations and refining his swing slightly, he was able to win a tour event.

The aphorism "Whether you think you can, or whether you think you can't, you're right" certainly is true for golfers. You just have to decide which way you're going to think. It's up to you.

CHAPTER SUMMARY

- Go to the "practice" tee, not the "driving" range.
- Quality practice time is more important than quantity. Practice smarter, not necessarily longer.
- Always practice hitting toward a target.
- Simulate realistic game conditions on the practice tee.
- Relax and take steps to handle first-tee jitters.
- Bring the appropriate expectations with you to the course.

CHAPTER 6

THE IMPORTANCE OF
A PRESHOT ROUTINE

When Payne Stewart and I began working together in 1988, he had all the shots, but his game lacked a preshot routine to enable his creative shotmaking ability to blossom on the highest level. In the intervening years, Payne has developed a sound preshot routine and this additional structure is one reason he has won major championships and proven himself as one of the world's finest golfers.

Without diminishing his creative shotmaking, the consistent use of a preshot routine, among other refinements, has allowed Payne to add a vital piece of the golf puzzle to his game. Just like Payne, if you're not aware of the benefit of a preshot routine, you're holding yourself back from being as good a player as you can be.

In short, a sound preshot routine is a series of physical and psychological steps taken by a golfer to prepare to hit the best possible shot of which he is capable. A good preshot routine should be a series of positive things to do. I never want to hear a golfer verbalize a preshot routine thought in the negative. There are enough negative pitfalls to watch out for in golf that you don't need to be preparing to play a shot while thinking negatively. Don't say, "There's a water hazard bordering the right side of the fairway; I sure don't want to miss this shot over there." Instead, use a positive thought such as, "This hole sets up best with a tee shot down the left-center of the fairway; that's where I want to drive the ball." Always think of playing to a safe landing area rather than playing away from trouble.

A preshot routine can be something for you to count on, regardless of where you are playing, how you are playing, or with whom you are playing. It can be a little bit like your best friend, a comfort in times of stress—a security blanket. Without a consistently performed, predictable preshot routine, you'll be at a disadvantage if you're up against a golfer who has one, particularly late in the round when the pressure is greatest. This is true whether the pressure is being caused by virtue of it being the club championship or the national open championship.

Routines can be seen throughout sports. In tennis, players bounce the ball a certain, exact number of times before serving. In football, placekickers note where the ball will be spotted and then pace off the approach steps that they will make toward the ball. In baseball, batters dig in their plant foot and take their practice swings in a consistent manner.

A preshot routine is the place to be a chess master, an opportunity for you to use a series of well-thought-out actions to put yourself in the best possible position to succeed once you take on the role of athlete and set the club in motion.

FIVE STEPS TO A SUCCESSFUL PRESHOT
ROUTINE

1. Signal yourself to enter the concentration zone. A sound preshot routine starts when you begin to totally focus your attention on the task at hand. This first step is especially important if you ride in a golf cart when you play, which can exacerbate the tendency to rush into a shot without first employing a thorough routine.

The signal can, and does, vary from player to player. Examples of effective signals with which to enter the concentration zone include opening and closing the Velcro snap of your golf glove; tugging on your belt or pants leg a certain number of times; touching the hosel of the club with your thumb and forefinger; tapping the club against the side of your shoe; pulling gently on the hair of your arm; running your fingers around a necklace; or tugging on your ear lobe or earring.

Regardless of the signal you choose, it needs to be a stimulus significant enough to draw your attention to what you're about to do. Stay away from using signals that already are merely habitual parts of your overall behavior. Arnold Palmer, for example, wouldn't want to use the hitching up of his slacks because he does this frequently on the course—and not just prior to settling in to play a shot.

If you're an individual who reacts more to sounds than the sense of touch, the signals involving the Velcro on your glove or tapping a club against your shoe might work best. The only sure way to see what type of signal works best for you is to experiment with several different ones. Once you've chosen your signal you must always honor it;

if someone or something breaks your concentration after you've signaled, break away, resignal, and start again.

2. Choose an intermediate target on your intended line of play. If you watch Jack Nicklaus play very much, you know that this is a key variable in his preshot preparation; Nicklaus can be seen picking his intermediate target when he is behind the ball and then turning his eyes toward it when he addresses the ball. In fact, most successful golfers employ this technique. Your intermediate aiming point can be a differently colored patch of grass, a leaf, an old divot, or a discarded cigarette butt. Keep in mind, however, that the rules of golf don't permit you to place any object on your intended target line. The mark has to already be on the ground when you get ready to play your shot. But remember, on each tee you have the ball in your hand, so you can choose an aiming spot and put your ball behind it at least eighteen times a round.

The most important consideration in choosing an intermediate target is that it be within your peripheral vision and that you be able to see your ball/clubface and the aiming point at the same time. To help me figure out how far away the intermediate aiming spot should be, I once tested about 150 golfers at their address positions. The average maximum peripheral vision among them was six feet. To avoid unnecessary difficulty in the event that your peripheral vision is less than average, pick an intermediate target some one and a half to two feet in front of your ball if possible.

Among the benefits of choosing and using an intermediate target is the reduction of tension associated with uncertain alignment. When you know, by the use of an aiming point, that you are aligned correctly to your target, you don't tend to wiggle and fidget as do golfers who aren't sure where they're aiming. If you're uncertain about a target, you tend to be quick on the backswing and the downswing, and other flaws can occur as well when your body instinctively tries to make moves to compensate for perceived faulty alignment. Proper use of an intermediate target can give you psychological comfort that can help the rhythm and tempo of your swing.

The first psychological moment of truth in the golf swing occurs when the player chooses and commits to a line of intended flight. This is when tension begins to build in the golfer. All of the previous movements do not cost the golfer anything if they are wrong. Practice swings at dandelions and cigar butts can be tension-free because they have no consequences. But if the golfer misaims his clubface to the ball, he instinctively knows that this mistake will cost something throughout the rest of the swing.

3. Take a diaphragmatic cleansing breath. If you don't think this makes any sense, then you've never seen the benefits of it when used to control muscle tension during natural childbirth techniques. A challenging shot on the golf course, even in a pressurized competitive setting, pales in comparison. Yet many players "forget to breathe" under the heat of competition. They literally hold their breath or take shallow gulps of air when faced with a tough shot. A good, cleansing breath serves to reduce tension as well as oxygenate the blood so that your muscles function efficiently. Opera singers are taught this diaphragmatic breath to improve their performance, just as athletes are. Watch free-throw shooters in basketball; they exhale just before releasing the shot.

As part of a preshot routine, your cleansing breath can occur either while you are behind your ball in the process of choosing an intermediate target or while you are at address. It is simply a matter of personal preference. Regardless of when you take your cleansing breath, make sure it's a deep diaphragm movement involving your entire upper torso.

4. Make a rehearsal, or tune-up, swing. Unlike a practice swing taken on the practice tee, which often centers on a mechanical or technical aspect, this rehearsal is an attempt to tune up the muscles and nerves to feel the appropriate movements during the swing. Think of it like a symphony orchestra tuning up before a concert. Or recall basketball player Cedric "Cornbread" Maxwell of UNC-Charlotte and the Boston Celtics, who used to go through his shooting motion without the ball each time he stepped to the foul line. He was rehearsing, not practicing; there's a big difference.

Of the rehearsal swings used by tour players, Corey Pavin's may look the most unorthodox because of the way he exaggerates keeping his right elbow tucked tightly to his side on the backswing. Pavin's real swing does not look like his tune-up swing, but by rehearsing and exaggerating the feeling that he wants his body to have, he is readying himself to make a good swing. Since he began using his exaggerated rehearsal swing, he rarely is plagued by getting too loose and having his right arm run too far away from his body on the backswing, which used to be a major cause of his bad shots.

Your particular rehearsal swing should, like Pavin's, help your body sense the way you want it to move during a real swing. A rehearsal swing is especially important if you have to hit a shot with a shape or trajectory which is not your normal one. Also, some courses, such as Augusta National, ask you to hit a certain shot (a draw) all around the course but suddenly, on the eighteenth tee, you are asked to hit a cut shot to have the optimum chance to put the ball in the right position to attack the pin. That's one of the reasons you see rehearsal swings on the eighteenth at Augusta by tour pros who ordinarily do not have this move in their preshot routines.

5. Give yourself a cue or thought which allows you to give up voluntary control of the swing and shift to involuntary action. As discussed in chapter 3, golf demands that you exhibit a split personality in order to play the game well. This concluding part of a sound preshot routine is that juncture in golf when you allow yourself to let go—to transform yourself from chess master to athlete. Failure to allow yourself to move from the analytic to intuitive modes of the game will usually result in ineffective, off-target shotmaking. We've all seen the outcome when we try to steer the putter on a four-foot putt or guide the club on a tee shot. Letting go of voluntary control can be very hard to do during pressure situations on the course. At these times, do your best to ensure that you carry out this final part of a preshot routine.

The second psychological moment of truth in a golf swing is this letting go of voluntary or conscious control and turning it over to involuntary or subconscious action. Some tour players have developed little reminder cues such as "Turn It Loose, Mother Goose," "Tee It High and Let It Fly," or "Grip and Rip" to help them handle this psychological moment of truth.

MAKING SURE YOUR ROUTINE
DOESN'T BECOME A RITUAL

As with most things in golf, too much of a good thing can spell trouble. As the sage instructor Harvey Penick says, "Just because one aspirin is good, you don't take the whole bottleful." A preshot routine that helps your game can turn into a preshot ritual that hurts it. I define *routine* as "a cognitively focused set of actions that are performed at a high level of conscious awareness and are systematic and purposeful in nature." In contrast, a *ritual* is "a set of repetitive actions which may have little cognitive purpose or awareness and that are often done at a low level of consciousness."

Rituals can take the form of a religious creed recited aloud with a congregation with little thought to or awareness of its meaning, or in the pledge of allegiance to the flag said without regard to the purpose of the pledge. Behaviors which begin as routines can become ritualized after much casual repetition.

I've seen golfers' preshot routines turn into rituals which lose their effectiveness and, in fact, cause more harm than good. This happens because of both casual repetition over time and the inclusion of too many steps in the routine. One LPGA player who sought my help was having a tough time being a consistent putter. When we first worked together, I asked her to go through what she normally did upon reaching a green until she stroked a putt. As she told me about her procedure, she walked three deliberate paces behind her ball, turned ninety degrees away from it, and made seven precise practice strokes. Upon walking back to her ball, she made three more practice strokes before finally hitting the putt. Questioned about her "routine," she admitted that as she stood over many putts, her mind was still on whether she had taken exactly seven practice strokes.

Always taking the exact number of putting strokes is a ritual, not a routine. I watched a good college golfer go through his preputt routine of three practice strokes. The problem was, for whatever reason, he struck his right foot with the putterhead during the third practice stroke. But because he was so stuck in his ritual, he went ahead and hit the putt after his third practice stroke without backing away to regain his composure. Needless to say, he did not sink that putt.

Another young LPGA player asked for my help because she was freezing over the ball, almost unable to begin her backswing. She eventually revealed that her swing instructor had advised her to go through a twelve-step preswing ritual that had to be completed in a time varying no more than one and a half seconds from shot to shot. The ritual drained her energy and when she got over the ball, seemingly prepared to finally play a shot, she was still focused on whether she had completed all of the dozen steps in the allotted time.

Those three players provide examples of good intentions gone very awry. The tail should not wag the dog; a preshot routine isn't the game, only an important part of it. To keep your routine from becoming either a reflexive or an excessive behavior, examine it periodically and make small adjustments to keep it fresh and viable. Changing the signal that you use to begin your routine is one possibility. If you've been using the Velcro on your glove, switch to a tug on your pants leg or belt. Or try a deliberate, conscious countdown such as "Three, two, one, go."

By all means, don't let your routine become too lengthy and too complex. The five steps outlined here are enough. If you've never used a preshot routine, the five steps may seem like they will take too much time. That's not the case, though, and you can find out by having a friend time your preshot routine on the practice tee. From the time you signal yourself to enter the concentration zone to the time you put the club in motion, it should take about thirty seconds. If you are found to be taking a great deal more than thirty seconds, examine your routine until you can accomplish it in a time close to a half a minute.

To sharpen your preshot routine, I recommend that you use it on every fifth shot during practice-tee sessions. Trying to use it more often on the practice tee is futile for most golfers, because in the rush to hit as many balls as they can, they skip elements and breed sloppy habits in the very area in which they are trying to establish precision and predictability. As long as you do your routine correctly, once every fifth shot is often enough—most golfers find this frequency demands about as much self-discipline as they can muster on the practice range.

On the course, though, never hit a shot without going through your preshot routine, no matter how casual a round it might be. But don't become discouraged if at first you're unable to perform it before every shot. An initial success rate of 75 percent of your shots is acceptable for someone who has just begun to integrate a preshot routine into his game. Work to improve this percentage in every successive round.

Keep in mind that a successful preshot routine is one that is carried out without interruption. If an outside factor such as a companion shouting across the fairway, a passing car honking its horn, or sudden gust of wind shakes your routine, stop and restart your routine. Good players understand this well and take pains to restart their routine rather than move through it after being interrupted. Billy Casper even asks his caddie to take back the club that he may have chosen, put the club back in the bag, and then tilt the bag at an angle so that he can restart his preshot routine by pulling the club out of his bag in the exact same fashion as he did the first time. When he backs off during a preshot routine, Payne Stewart often takes a towel and wipes off the grip of his club, whether or not the grip is damp. This gives him time to settle back into his signal and restart his routine.

Of all the areas in which average golfers try to emulate the best golfers in the world, this is one in which the search to copy actually can succeed. You don't have to have the mind or the body of a tour pro to make a sound preshot routine a consistent part of your game. Like the tour pro, however, you must be diligent and willing to put forth the effort. If you succeed, you will have gained control of the part of golf that needs structure and be well on your way to becoming a disciplined shotmaker. Performing a sound preshot routine won't give you all the shots, but it is the best way for you to prepare to give your all on every one of them.

CHAPTER SUMMARY

- A preshot routine is the disciplined part of golf in which you put yourself in the best possible position, both physically and psychologically, to hit the best shot of which you are capable.
- A preshot routine consists of physical and psychological components, all positive in nature.
- Keep your preshot routine as simple as possible, performed in about thirty seconds.
- Beware of a beneficial routine turning into a harmful ritual.
- Try to never play a shot on the course without first going through your preshot routine.
- A preshot routine demands no particular physical talent; it does require diligence, effort, and self-discipline.

CHAPTER 7

UNDERSTANDING AND DEVELOPING CONCENTRATION

I n addition to the gulf that exists between the physical skills of golf's top players and the rest of us, there is another huge difference. Skilled golfers talk about "being in the zone," "being in the cocoon," "being focused," "getting good pictures," and "being on automatic pilot." They are attempting to describe concentration, an area in which they excel but many amateurs do not. Far too many weekend golfers think that concentration is just an old television game show.

This is unfortunate, because concentration is an area in which average golfers legitimately have a chance to match the professionals. Concentration demands no extraordinary strength, flexibility, or finely tuned coordination. And it is the nature of golf itself that, with no opponent trying to block your shots, tackle you, or, for that matter, return your serve, no sport rewards concentration so directly.

Concentration is a difficult thing to pinpoint, even for those golfers who do it well on the course. They usually resort to describing it with the phrases and slogans above, rather than with a concrete definition. For more definitive language, psychologists who have studied the thought patterns of skilled athletes do a better job.

Dr. Michael Mahoney, a psychologist who has studied concentration in athletes for several years, says, "To concentrate means to center, to become totally absorbed or focused on a specific point, task, or theme of action, free from any irrelevant internal or external distractions, yet tuned in to those cues most relevant to peak performance."

Dr. Mike Csikszentmihalyi, a psychologist who specializes in the state of concentration called "flow," emphasizes the ability to be "fully absorbed in the activity at hand, with attention finely attuned to the shifting demands of the moment." In Csikszentmihalyi's studies, he found similar patterns of "flow states" in athletes, dancers, chess masters, rock climbers, surgeons, and composers. When the individuals were concentrating, they experienced a distortion in their sense of time. Events seemed to pass very quickly or very slowly. In addition, he found that during the flow state of concentration there is "an altered sense of one's bodily sensations or sensory perceptions, and a fine precision in gauging one's response to a changing challenge."

After working with professional golfers for seventeen years and researching the subject thoroughly, I've concluded that concentration in golf is probably more difficult than in any other sport. This is so mainly because two different types of concentration must occur on every shot. The first—disciplined concentration—is the golfer as chess master. The second—flow concentration—is the golfer as athlete.

Disciplined concentration occurs during all of a golfer's preswing thought processes. It concerns aiming at a target, alignment of the body to the intended line of flight, body posture, preshot routine, analysis of course conditions, and gauging the effects of the weather on the shot. Generally, it is an ever-present awareness of the continually changing environment faced on the course—from tee to fairway to bunker to green to tee, again and again. The word *disciplined* is used because this type of concentration involves many preswing factors which most golfers consider boring and therefore have to force themselves to take care of. Mundane or not, they can wreck your scorecard if you don't give them proper attention.

You can directly control your level of disciplined concentration. Much of this control depends on how "mentally tough" you are. Those two words get a lot of use in sports, but I define mental toughness as "the ability to consistently control the mental, emotional, and physical response to situations in which there are stimuli that produce high levels of distraction, stress, or tension." You have to gain control of your thought processes and apply the effort to take care of the "boring" aspects of the game. Consistent disciplined concentration is obtainable by every golfer regardless of size, strength, sex, or handicap level.

Flow concentration is more subconscious in nature, involving the intuitive portion of the game that exists during the swing. Flow concentration is much harder for a golfer to achieve consistently than disciplined concentration. Better flow concentration can be assisted by focusing more on the process than on the product—if you worry less about the outcome. Think about letting the green catch your shots rather than trying to force your shots onto the green.

"Nothing interferes with performance like concentrating on the goal rather the process of one's game," says Tim Strickland, a professional archery teacher. "An archer who worries about his score will try to make his arrows go in instead of letting them go in. If your technique is correct, the target never enters your mind. It's just there to catch your arrows. Oriental archers learn this way, but Americans are not trained with the same thought patterns. They're always thinking about the score."

If you've ever enjoyed any success at darts or archery, you may have sensed the feeling that the bull's-eye was "just getting in the way." I once saw some evidence that this feeling may transfer to golf when I had the occasion to play darts with Corey Pavin and Paul Azinger. Paul, who was bothered with a injury to his right shoulder at the time, threw well enough left-handed to blow me away. Afterward, he said that as a kid he had aspired to be a world-class darts player—he wasn't bad as a part-timer! Azinger has an innate sense of hand-eye coordination that transfers to golf and helps make him one of the best shotmakers in the game. It's not unusual to discover that tour golfers are usually good at shooting pool, throwing darts, or shooting skeet. Many excelled at other sports when they were children and teenagers before turning their full attention toward golf.

It's important to understand that during the swing you should be allocating different levels of attention to a variety of factors. For example, some level of your concentration needs to be on the target, even if this is only to allow it to catch your ball. On this level, called "orientation," you know where you want the ball to land but aren't totally focused on the target. On the second level, "awareness concentration," you are concentrating on the ball but not fixated on it. The better player is aware of the ball only enough to allow his club to find it. In a sense, the ball only gets in the way of the swing. The third factor that needs some concentration during the swing is the swinging motion itself. The "feel" of the swing and the position of the clubhead are where most good players apportion the greatest amount of their concentration. They truly focus on this swing sense; they emphasize feel over mechanics.

Does your level of flow concentration increase as you become a better golfer? Dr. Monte Buchsbaum, a psychiatrist at the University of California, Irvine, studied expert video-game players and found a marked decrease in the brain's overall metabolic rate during periods of intense concentration. The inference is that the more skill a person brings to a task, the more efficiently his brain operates.

As a person masters a skill, brain activity decreases except in one area: the visual cortex. This part of the brain, which processes visual imagery, shows an increase in metabolic rate as a person acquires greater skill. Buchsbaum asserts that this is because the person is able to process more visual information as his skill increases. The increased efficiency of this type of information processing may help us to achieve flow concentration more often.

In golf, visual imagery is a big part of flow concentration, allowing skilled players to "get good pictures" during play. We'll examine the entire realm of visualization in chapter 8.

To recap the differences between the two types of concentration, consider the following:

Disciplined concentration—Awareness of events, objects, and movement is highly conscious. Thought is rational, strategic, systematic, and detail-oriented. The thought process is static, result-oriented, analytical, external, and focuses on one detail at a time.

Flow concentration—Awareness is mostly subconscious. Thought is creative, intuitive, feel-dominated, and visually oriented. The thought process is dynamic, process-oriented, integrative, and internal, with simultaneous attention paid to several variables.

Exercising Your Concentration Skills

Although many of golf's mental skills need to be honed on the practice tee or course, you can increase your ability to concentrate in the comfort of your living room or den. The following exercises, done properly, will help you learn to quiet your mind and gently guide it back to focus rather than trying to force yourself to concentrate—the latter approach usually doesn't work well for golfers of any handicap level. Approach the exercises with an open mind; they'll help if you give them a chance.

To begin, sit down in a comfortable chair in a quiet room in which you're not likely to be interrupted. Remove a new golf ball from your bag, and look at it as if it were the first ball you've ever seen. Note the brand name of the ball. See if you can determine where the hemispheres of the ball are joined. Look at the dimple patterns.

Learn to look at the ball without becoming fixated on it. When you find yourself staring at the ball without seeing it, you are no longer concentrating. Shift your focus and restart your concentration.

Examine the logo on the ball. Note the size of the print. What color is the number? When you feel your concentration wandering, take note of where your attention is shifting. Does your mind go back in time? Toward the future? Is there any pattern to your thoughts? Do you believe you lose concentration because you lose interest in the task or because there are outside distractions?

Now turn your attention back to the ball. Then look away. Visually re-create each aspect of the ball in your mind, including the color of the print on the ball. Look once more at the ball. How well did you do in visualizing it? Repeat this exercise with some light, instrumental music playing in the background. Is it harder to sustain concentration with the music on than when you were sitting in absolute quiet? Where does your mind tend to wander when you have the music playing? Now repeat the exercise while listening to music that has lyrics. Is it harder to concentrate? Where does your mind wander now?

Later in the day, repeat the exercise using an object more complex than a golf ball. Choose a magazine cover, painting, or similar object. The entire process shouldn't take more than ten minutes or so. After a few days of using these exercises, you should be able to sustain your concentration for longer periods of time, even with the distractions. When you play golf the next time out, you should be able to notice an improved ability to concentrate.

AVOIDING THE THREATS THAT CAN HINDER CONCENTRATION

Pressure. Under the heat of competition, golfers tend to fail to process all the relevant details necessary for disciplined preparation. These omissions may involve poor strategy or bad club selection. Conscious thought may freeze up. Pressure also can hinder flow concentration because a certain amount of relaxation is necessary in order for flow to occur. Relaxation techniques practiced off the course may help in this regard.

Anxiety. A similar but not identical threat is anxiety. Anxious golfers do not necessarily have to be playing in a tense, competitive situation. Anxiety can plague any golfer when he is out to prove himself too much by interrupting his flow state of concentration and making him too product-oriented. He becomes so worried about his score (product) that he forgets to focus on the process that produces the score.

In a broader sense, Payne Stewart had this problem earlier in his career after he had recorded quite a few runner-up finishes and had not yet achieved the expectations that others held for him. Many people were telling him to "win more," and he started to focus on more victories without working on the process (improved play) that ultimately would lead him to the success that he subsequently was able to achieve once he became more process-oriented.

Comfort zones. This threat to concentration afflicts all golfers, but amateurs seeking to break 100, 90, or 80 for the first time seem to suffer the most. Coming to the eighteenth hole needing a par for a personal scoring best causes many players to lose their focus. Fighting to break out of a comfort zone, golfers often must overcome a potent mixture of anxiety and pressure.

In breaking through a comfort zone, one of the most helpful strategies is to remember that all golfers have had the problem at one point or another in their career. It also helps to break through your comfort zones in realistic steps; don't expect to make a quantum leap in scoring. If you're trying to break 80 for the first time, for example, you should expect to shoot 80, 81, or 82 several times before you finally accomplish your goal.

Unfamiliar courses and playing companions. When most amateurs set foot on a new—and in particular, marquee—course after much anticipation, neither disciplined nor flow concentration works well for them. They succumb to their nerves and too much adrenaline. Tour professionals have the opposite response when they visit a famous course: an inspired layout often causes their concentration to flow much better than it does when they play an ordinary course.

When paired with different and/or more talented playing companions, pros and amateurs both can suffer diminished concentration skills. When you find yourself paired with a much better golfer, you should understand that you're not under a microscope. Your companion is a good player partly because he stays focused on his game, not anybody else's.

Boredom. If you play a lot of golf, this is a greater threat to you than to someone who doesn't play as often. Retirees and tour professionals—individuals who have the opportunity to play frequently, if they choose—are most likely to be affected. Most golfers don't get the chance to play enough to become bored, but pros who compete in six consecutive tour events become what they term "brain dead." Their disciplined concentration disappears because they've been through so much preshot preparation in so many competitive rounds that they reach the point of just going through the motions instead of making active decisions. Boredom also leads to playing without the feel, creativity, and mental imagery that are necessary for flow concentration.

For skilled golfers, boredom can result on particular shots that are viewed as unchallenging. I worked with one player who had a lot of trouble on those "plain vanilla" shots. If he was faced with a simple 8-iron to an unguarded green, he often would lose his focus and mishit the shot. To solve the problem, I asked him to make certain that he attempted to play a certain-shaped shot, draw or fade, even though the conditions didn't demand it. The concentration he achieved by turning the ball one way or the other more than made up for it being a more difficult shot.

Outside distractions. As you'll learn if you practice the concentration exercises discussed earlier in the chapter, outside distractions affect you according to how effectively you are concentrating. Sometimes when we play, a construction worker at a homesite next to the course may hammer as loudly as he can and we're hardly aware of it. The next day, the chirp of a bird can pierce our concentration.

While you can't eliminate outside noises or other disturbances, you can try to keep yourself from being bothered simply by not giving permission for it to happen. I worked with a college golfer who learned this lesson during a tournament in which he was paired with Jack Nicklaus's son, Gary Nicklaus. The player began fantastically with a birdie and an eagle on the first two holes. Standing on the third tee, though, he noticed a helicopter landing nearby—it was Jack arriving to watch Gary. By the end of the front nine, the player had given up seven strokes and gone from three under par to four over. While Jack Nicklaus had done nothing to distract the young player—he hadn't talked during his backswing or jingled coins while he putted—the golfer had *allowed* Nicklaus's presence to bother him.

If the collegian learned his lesson well, he will act more like Jack Nicklaus, Tom Watson, and other champions who successfully tune out potential distractions during play. It is no coincidence that the great players, with a few exceptions, seem to block out the movement of television crews or gallery marshals much better than their less-successful colleagues.

If they can't block distractions, they seek to control them. One tour player was getting very unsettled by a miked television cameraman who followed closely in search of a comment. The player never knew where this fellow was going to be next, so to control the situation, he made a point to give the camera some friendly words. Television had the comments it was after, and the player didn't have to worry about the "up close and personal" camera affecting his concentration for the rest of the tournament.

A lack of confidence. When talking to numerous tour players about concentration, it came as somewhat of a surprise when nearly all of them noted that a lack of confidence had eroded their concentration skills at some point. The consensus was that when they began to play poorly, they tended to concentrate less, and when their concentration slipped, they began to play even worse. It was a vicious circle.

No one can expect to play his best all of the time, of course, but proper preparation can bolster your confidence and keep your concentration from waning in any case. Aware that he would miss some greens and face some up-and-down situations from tall rough at the 1991 U.S. Open, Payne Stewart spent several days at home in the week preceding the championship working on just such shots. It paid off as he won the Open, thanks in part to a couple of crucial up-and-downs in the closing moments. For similar reasons, many of the top golfers with an eye toward the U.S. Open have chosen in recent years to play the week before the national championship in the tour event at the Westchester Country Club in Harrison, New York, a testy layout with tough roughs and slick greens similar to an Open venue.

The relationship between confidence and flow concentration in sports was pointed out in the summer of 1986 when I played a round of golf with Michael Jordan a couple of weeks after he had scored sixty-three points in a playoff game against the Boston Celtics, one of the best individual efforts in NBA history. He told me that in that game he had been in such a zone, brimming with such confidence, that he didn't think the opposition could touch him. He recalled that he hadn't been aware of the game score or how many points he was accumulating. Jordan had been lost in the process of the game. He was doing, not thinking, thanks in part to his great confidence in his ability. At that time, Jordan was still a newcomer to golf, not very confident in his talent, and as a result wasn't able to establish such a high degree of flow concentration in his second sport.

TO GRIND OR NOT TO GRIND

Because golf is a sport of initiating rather than reacting to action, with relatively large chunks of time between shots, how do you concentrate throughout a round? You have two choices: to take the approach of total, uninterrupted concentration for the whole four hours or so of play, or to focus on a shot, turn your mind off, then refocus for the next shot until the round is completed.

The strategy of unbroken concentration—called *zanshin* by the Japanese—is best exemplified by Ben Hogan, whose career is recounted by both true and apocryphal stories of his *zanshin*. One story has Hogan's wife, Valerie, coming up to within a couple of feet of her husband during a round and speaking to him; afterward, Hogan couldn't remember seeing her. Another tale involves Hogan's playing partner, Claude Harmon, acing the twelfth hole at Augusta and Hogan walking onto the next tee and asking him what he'd just made.

Jack Nicklaus provides the most prominent example of a golfer choosing to go into focus, relax, and then refocusing for the next shot. On the golf course, Nicklaus is transferring an ability he has in other areas of his life to shift and reestablish his focus at will.

For Nicklaus, this ability exists even—and maybe especially—during the biggest competitions. Veteran golf writer Al Barkow recalls that during the thick of the 1972 British Open Championship, with Nicklaus in hot pursuit of the third leg of the modern Grand Slam, the Golden Bear was walking within earshot when Barkow noted to another reporter that the turf on the Muirfield links was "harder than a New York sidewalk." Nicklaus replied that it was even harder than that, then went about the business of golf. At another British Open, Nicklaus got to the green of a particular hole and realized that the shape and slope of the putting surface was one that he wanted to use in a future course design of his own. Pulling paper and pen out of his golf bag, he sketched the green then and there.

It should be rather obvious that the majority of golfers will be better served to approach the game as Nicklaus does, instead of trying to grind their way around the course in the manner made famous by Hogan.

Foremost, golf is meant to be enjoyed, and much of the pleasure comes from the interaction with playing companions during those many minutes between shots. To miss out on this camaraderie is to cheat yourself of one of golf's principal allures—you'll also be pretty unpopular with your playing companions if you give them the silent treatment all the way around.

From a practical standpoint, accomplishing tasks between interruptions is how most of the world operates today. Business executives rarely get to spend long periods of time concentrating on one thing. People with busy lives are used to working at one project, putting it aside, and then working again on it later. In that sense, the Nicklaus approach mirrors society at large. Moreover, devotees of the *zanshin* approach usually find themselves physically and mentally fatigued by the time they get to the fifteenth or sixteenth hole and it is difficult to post good scores feeling that way. For this reason, the overwhelming percentage of successful top-level golfers utilize the focus-relax-refocus strategy of concentration.

Those golfers who feel that they must stick to a *zanshin* approach or else risk losing all ability to concentrate are misguided. If you have a signal that you use to enter the concentration zone as the first step of a good preshot routine (see chapter 6), and you faithfully honor that signal, you can play well without grinding your way around. This is not to say that you should adopt another personality type in order to play this way—it's not necessary to be a jokester, just be human. Another important thing to remember if you adopt the Nicklaus approach is to keep your thoughts between shots light and casual. Don't fret about your child's grades or how much your new roof is going to cost.

ACHIEVING REALISTIC, EFFECTIVE CONCENTRATION

One of the most valuable lessons is to be aware of when you are not concentrating. If you mess up a shot and say after the fact that you weren't concentrating, it is too late. I try to encourage the golfers that I work with to learn to read their thought processes and body reactions so that they can recognize their lack of concentration before they make a mistake. This is not easy to do, but if you can figure out when you're starting to "blank out," as many golfers term it, you will save strokes.

Among the questions I am asked the most is, What should I concentrate on, feel or mechanics? The answer is, If at all possible, think about feel while on the course.

Use mechanics as a last resort. Golfers and other athletes usually are playing by feel when they're at their best. When they're enjoying a peak performance, concentration is one part of the 3-C recipe: if you play with Composure, Confidence, and Concentration, the rest will follow.

On those days when everything isn't going right, you may need to concentrate more on mechanics until your feel returns. If you're a higher-handicap golfer, you may need to concentrate more on mechanics until your technique improves some. If you're unable to improve the physical part of your game, you will have a more difficult time playing by feel—but this doesn't mean you should never attempt to do so. You will have days—indeed, you probably already have experienced them—when you're "on your game" just as the tour pro has days when he is on his. Just because there is a gap between your scores doesn't mean you should become discouraged.

Dr. Michael Mahoney suggests that athletes learn to concentrate by focusing on three things: (1) positive thoughts, (2) the current event, and (3) positive self-suggestions that stress proper form and execution.

For golfers, Mahoney's first point means thinking about the shape of the shot you ought to hit in order to have the ball reach a certain target rather than where you don't want the ball to go. Focusing on the current event refers to every golfer's strong temptation for the mind to wander to a hole past or a hole ahead—either is troublesome. Concerning the third area of focus, you have plenty of opportunities to speak to yourself on the course (self-talk will be addressed in full in chapter 11). The pace of golf, in fact, may allow participants more of an opportunity to do this than athletes in any other sport. Cues such as "low and slow," "turn and stretch," and "clear the left side" stress proper technique. Used appropriately, the cues are part of an effective preshot routine that can put you in a positive frame of mind.

As with many of golf's mental challenges, to concentrate at maximum effectiveness means to tax your mind. When Payne Stewart was playing in the 1991 U.S. Open and 1990 British Open, I knew he was concentrating well because in every one of our postround meetings he told me that he had a "good headache." It's a simple yet effective gauge. Despite how well he was concentrating, however, Payne was unable to totally concentrate at 100 percent on all his shots. No golfer, even on the highest level of competition, ever can. The mind simply is not a machine, and we aren't robots.

Nonetheless, many amateurs have an unrealistic notion about how effectively tour players are able to concentrate. When a tour pro comes to me for help, one of the first things I do is ask him to rate the extent to which he truly concentrated during his four most recent tournaments; we develop a concentration scorecard for each round. The pros who answer honestly report that they enjoyed full concentration on only 65 to 70 percent of their shots. When they judge their concentration to be at its best, tour players offer varying views as to how many of their shots they devote full concentration to. The estimates range from 75 to 98 percent of their shots. Some players are harder graders than others.

These percentages, of course, are for the best players in the world. For you, how often you are able to achieve full concentration depends on your level of physical and mental talent, how often you play, and the effort you apply toward concentrating keenly. A more thorough understanding of concentration, which you should have now, certainly will help. And when you do have one of those rounds in which you are "in the zone," savor it. The days when both disciplined and flow concentration are at peak level are few for any golfer. It is certain, however, that the better you concentrate, the better you will play—regardless of your handicap.

Chapter Summary

- Good concentration skills are within reach of all golfers but are achieved by only a few.
- Golf requires both disciplined and flow concentration. Effort and exercises can increase disciplined concentration ability; peak flow concentration is more elusive but it is helped by decreasing anxiety and increasing confidence.
- Be aware of the numerous factors that can threaten your concentration, including boredom, outside distractions, anxiety, and a lack of confidence.
- For best results, concentrate hard on every shot but relax between them. Don't try to "grind" your way around the course.
- Be realistic about how thoroughly you concentrate. Even golf's best players are unable to achieve full concentration on 100 percent of their shots.

CHAPTER

VISUALIZATION:
SEEING YOURSELF SUCCEED

To get you in the appropriate frame of mind to consider visualization in golf, I want you to recall the times that you've successfully escaped trouble on the course by hitting shots that seemingly were beyond your ability level. The times when you were able to punch the ball low enough to avoid overhanging limbs, or curve the ball one way or the other around obstacles that stood in your target path.

When you had gotten the ball out safely into the fairway or onto the green from those unlikely situations, you probably gave yourself a well-deserved psychological pat on the back and moved on—pleased with the outcome but a little bit perplexed as to how you pulled off the shot. Other factors may have contributed to your successfully hitting those trouble shots, but it's almost certain that the main reason you rose to the occasion is because the situation forced you to visualize the shot in your mind before pulling the trigger. You were forced to do on those trouble shots what good golfers regularly do on all their strokes. In those infrequent moments—when those branches and trees framed where your ball needed to travel—you got the help that you needed in order to experience "seeing" a shot before you played it.

Visualization has become a catchword in sports psychology during the last decade. While nearly all contemporary sports psychologists agree that it is beneficial to athletes, many would-be pupils have viewed the concept as a one-step cure-all—the secret elixir of golf psychology. I don't see visualization as a magic-hat solution to all of a golfer's woes. But there is no doubt it can be a powerful tool. Research on the matter is continuing, but when a tour golfer says that he can't even "get good pictures" before he plays shots, and he blames his "bad pictures" for a slump, that is potent evidence for the argument that seeing is achieving in golf.

Like most areas of golf psychology, a person's ability to visualize can't be measured with a yardstick, and an onlooker can't ascertain what your mind is seeing before you play a shot. You alone can know that. That's why a knowledge of visualization is so important—so you can "screen" your mental pictures and make them work for you. Let's first examine the use of visualization on individual shots.

SEEING THE SHOT YOU WANT TO HIT

Before you play any shot, you need to have a mental picture of how you want the ball to react once you deliver the clubhead to the ball. You need to have a definite, positive visualization of what your shot will look like. This picture should indicate the trajectory, the direction, the spot where you intend the ball to land, and how far you want the ball to roll when it lands.

Many golfers have a difficult time visualizing these factors. It's only when they are in trouble, when the tree branches and tree trunks *literally* frame their shot for them that they are able to do so. Well, you don't have to be in the woods in order to visualize golf shots. But you do have to make more of an effort. When playing ordinary shots, visualize images to substitute for the literal frames that exist to help when you're playing trouble shots. If you're in a situation that calls for a low shot, visualize those overhanging branches in order to help yourself hit the low shot that's needed. If you have trouble defining a landing area for your shot, use the images of a soccer net or football goalposts. If the flight of a shot is difficult for you to picture, try visualizing a strip of highway that curves in the manner that you wish your ball to travel. Your options in this form of visualization are limited only by your imagination. You may see the green as a pin cushion ready to accept your shot. Someone else may see a dartboard. Still another golfer may visualize an archery target. Pick visual images that work for you. Visualization is one of the most individual aspects of golf psychology.

To improve your ability to visualize your shots, work on it during practice sessions. This is another reason practicing with a target in mind is critical. The practice area is the place to experiment with different visual images, until you find ones that are effective for you.

Getting good pictures of shots before you play them is another way of keeping negative thoughts out of your game. As discussed in the chapter on preshot routines, negative thoughts do you no good as you prepare to play a shot. Visualizing a successful shot—and not seeing your ball flying into the water or out of bounds—keeps you in a positive orientation. A "blank" mind can be just as deleterious as a negative one. While scientists still are not certain whether there is such a thing as a "blank" mind, don't take the chance of negative thoughts popping up by being noncommittal before a shot. If you approach each shot intent on showing yourself a positive mental movie of it before you hit it, you'll give yourself the best chance to hit the best shot of which you are capable. Jack Nicklaus said that he ran the movie of the shot both forward and backward before he hit the shot. This rewinding of the shot may help some people but confuse others.

TRANSLATING YOUR MENTAL MOVIE
INTO ANOTHER VISUAL PICTURE

This is the second level of visualization. It concerns the translation of the movie of the shot in your mind into a visualization of how your body parts will move (what your swing will be like) in order to hit such a shot. This visualization involves a person's proprioceptive-kinesthetic system, which, in essence, means the linkage of the body's muscles and nerves. This is probably as close as you can get to defining "feel" in golf. In this visualization, a golfer is presetting the feel that he wants to have in his body when he plays the shot. The mind's-eye visualization is translated into a type of neuromuscular representation of the shot.

When Sam Snead was asked how he hit a draw, he replied, "Ah just thinks draw." What he meant was that he saw a draw-shaped shot in his mind and then translated this picture into a draw swing. It's that simple for the great players.

The second level of visualization is something that all the great shotmakers possess. In fact, it is probably difficult to reach golf's highest level without it. All tour-caliber golfers enjoy it to some degree. And when golfers ask me to help them improve their games, one of the first things I attempt to find out is whether they possess this ability. If they don't, I know that there is a ceiling in the game that they won't be able to crack. The best performers in any sport are the ones with keen proprioceptive-kinesthetic systems.

USING THE SWINGS OF OTHERS TO HELP YOURSELF

If you've attended a PGA or LPGA Tour event and found that your own swing seemed to contain a little more rhythm and tempo than usual the next time you played, it was no accident. By watching the tour professionals swing their clubs with the proper pace, you were able to absorb some of their talent and it showed in your own game. This is common for many golfers of all talent levels. Even the most disjointed golfer begins to look rhythmical after observing smooth swingers such as Mark O'Meara, Gene Littler, or Nancy Lopez. The problem is that the newfound tempo doesn't last very long unless you're able to reinforce your visualization by regularly watching the tour pros.

Since few people can follow the tours week after week,

you need to find another way to retain the benefits of observing good golf swings. Fortunately, thanks to the video age we live in, you can use the swing images of good golfers to help correct mechanical flaws in your swing and to develop some of their fluid rhythm and tempo. If you go about this strategy systematically, it can have a definite positive impact on your game.

First, see a qualified PGA teaching professional and ask him to determine the aspects of your swing that need the most help. If you're like most golfers, you'll be plagued by two or three faults that you repeat over and over. When these flaws have been identified, ask your pro to recommend tour players who are very good at the parts of the swing you need to improve. If your instructor tells you that you have little leg action in your swing or don't use your legs properly, he might suggest you look closely at Jack Nicklaus, who uses his lower body very well.

Regardless of which particular area you need to improve, there are tour pros who will be appropriate models to observe. In some cases, the tour pro will appear to exaggerate the move that you need to work on. This is okay—perhaps even preferred—because in the learning process it's often necessary to overdo an image in order to make a significant change. (On the lesson tee, for example, your pro may tell you to feel as if all your weight were being transferred to your right foot on the backswing. With such a thought in mind, you may just be beginning to make a moderate shift to the right.) Furthermore, your mind will pick up a general sense of the proper move, not an exact replica.

The following list consists of examples of swing faults accompanied by the names of players whose swing image may help you eliminate a particular problem. Your pro will be able to assist you in customizing a list to fit your needs. If you're a woman or senior, you may relate more to LPGA or Senior PGA Tour players and choose to include more of them on your list.

YOUR SWING FAULT	PLAYER TO WATCH
Not Enough Leg Action	Jack Nicklaus
Incomplete Backswing	Payne Stewart
Rushed Downswing	Curtis Strange
Lack of Balance	Seve Ballesteros
Jerky Putting Stroke	Ben Crenshaw, Nancy Lopez
Poor Extension on Takeaway	Davis Love III, Tom Weiskopf
Failure to Transfer Weight from Rear Foot to Front Foot during Downswing	Greg Norman
Lack of Movement to Trigger Backswing	Lee Trevino, Mark Calcavecchia
Bad "Hands" on Pitch or Chip Shots	Paul Azinger, Lanny Wadkins

Once you have your list of the skills you need to develop and the tour pros you need to emulate, start videotaping players. You don't need a video camera; there is so much televised golf these days that you ought to be able over time to record the swings from telecasts and build a good library of swings. Make a special tape of repeated swings of players you need to observe. Don't attempt to *analyze* a player's moves when you watch, but try instead to develop an overall swing image that remains in your mind, much like the afterimage you get when you look at a bright neon sign and then close your eyes.

As your swing changes, you probably will need to choose the moves of other players to emphasize in your game. But don't despair if it takes several weeks, or even months, for this visualization process to work. On the positive side, keep in mind that using images in this fashion will speed up the learning process for most golfers. This is also a very effective way to teach golf to your children because they learn well through imitation.

Your personalized instruction tape will allow you to work on your game if poor weather keeps you from being outside. If you know that you're not going to be able to visit the practice range before an important match or tournament, you can pop the tape in your VCR the night before and get a feel for the swing you want to make. This can keep you from being burdened with too many mechanical swing thoughts.

If you want to carry this form of visualization to the next level, and you have access to a video recorder, produce a tape of your own good swings and view them much as you would one of the Sybervision instruction videos, which show the swing of a tour golfer over and over. When assembling your swings on tape, it's best to work with your pro to ensure that only good swings get on tape. You want your tape to be a personal highlights film, not a collection of bloopers.

RECALL PAST SUCCESS TO BUILD A GOOD PICTURE

In a similar vein, don't be shy about recalling your past successes achieved during actual play to help you with visualization. Regardless of skill level, every golfer has experienced successful moments on the course. That's really one of the game's calling cards. We might not be able to repeat those wonderful moments that we've enjoyed as consistently as we would like, but we've all had them, and there is nothing to stop us from recalling what they looked like and felt like.

The photo album in your golf memory might include a round in which you putted so true that you needed only twenty-five putts; a 4-iron that flew high and true to give you a gimme birdie on a brute of a par-4; a sand wedge shot blasted from an impossibly deep bunker to allow you to save par; a drive that soared farther and straighter than you ever imagined. If you're able to vividly recall triumphant moments such as those, draw on your memory both in introspective quiet moments off the course when you are contemplating your game, and during actual rounds when you face a similar shot to the one in your past.

Among the edges that champion golfers possess in crucial junctures during tournaments is that vision of their past successes. For Jack Nicklaus, the six-time winner of the Masters, there probably isn't a place on the Augusta National course from which he hasn't hit a memorable shot during more than thirty years of competition. This is one reason he's still likely to be in contention to win the Masters even though he is now over fifty years old.

You might well be in a similar position on your home

course; some golfers with fairly high handicaps have been known to post impressive ringer scores in the 50s over years of play. Those ringer scores result from wonderful shots which you can visualize from your memory.

Sharpening your ability to visualize isn't a panacea for all that might trouble your game, nor is it as simple as popping a tape into a VCR. Of the two distinct levels of visualization that occur each time you get ready to play a shot, the first level (picturing the flight and path of the shot that you're about to hit) is much easier to achieve than the second level (visualizing how your body is going to feel and move in order to send the ball on its intended course). There is no purpose served in deceiving yourself in this regard; the better player you are, the greater likelihood that you will be able to achieve the second level of visualization.

If you are able to visualize a shot, integrate the feel into your body, and then pull it off successfully, though, you've had a taste of being a shotmaker. There is no prettier picture in the game—it's golf at the highest level.

CHAPTER SUMMARY

- The best golfers achieve two levels of visualization on every shot. The first is a mental movie of the way they want the ball to fly; the second is a translation of that picture into an image of how their body should move in order to hit the shot.
- Incorporating the swing images of appropriate tour pros can help your visualization process.
- Recall your past successes to build good mental pictures.

EMOTIONAL TRAPS:
OVERCOMING FEAR AND ANGER

O f all the emotions that golf can elicit, the twin worries of fear and anger seem to cause the most problems for golfers. It is an intriguing pair of emotions as well. While most every golfer has banged a club on the ground or cursed in anger, not as many players are aware of the effect that fear has in golf. In fact, both emotions pose challenges to the psychological health of your game, in ways that you may never have imagined.

BELIEVE IT OR NOT, GOLF IS A SCARY SPORT

At first thought, golf wouldn't seem to be an endeavor rife with fear. It would seem, logically so, that a sports psychologist would spend a lot of time talking about fear when working with downhill skiers, divers, football players, or auto racers. Each of these sports presents a clear and constant threat to the physical well-being of the participant. But do golfers worry about fear? Interestingly, the topic of fear is often discussed when I work with both amateur and professional golfers, from the best to the worst. The source and manifestation of fear differs greatly from golfers to the athletes in the more outwardly daring sports, but the topic is nonetheless very real.

Unlike many other athletes, golfers rarely fear for their safety in regard to physical pain or injury, although a number of players have had their careers shortened as a result of injuries, and many play with much physical pain. Yet most golfers fear psychological factors, not physical ones. Many established tour players, for example, have a fear of losing their games and falling back into mediocrity. This may be the result of the nature of the game itself—with all its vagaries and small margin of error—or it can come from the large number of new, young, talented golfers who are just waiting to knock the established players off their pedestals. As a larger "new breed" of talent comes out of college each year, this threat has increased, with veteran tour players admitting that it's much tougher to win—and win repeatedly—these days.

Interviewed in *Esquire* magazine in November 1991, former football quarterback Terry Bradshaw presented this case succinctly in discussing his view of Joe Montana's insecurities. "You'd never believe it watching him play," Bradshaw said, "but Joe's got the insecurity that great artists have. They look so great to us from the outside. We place them on a pedestal, and we think they could never fall off. But they're always afraid they're gonna fall off. After all they've accomplished, they feel the opposite of the way we think they should feel. That insecurity has been a driving force for Joe Montana as much as his love for playing the damn game."

The fear that leads to insecurity that leads to motivation for playing the game at an ever-higher level applies to today's champion golfers as much as it does to Joe Montana. In fact, the linkage of fear, insecurity, and motivation is often mentioned in discussions of golf greats such as Ben Hogan, Sam Snead, and Byron Nelson. Lesser golfers felt the same fear. With these older golfers, much of the fear stemmed from their humble beginnings in life. Hogan sold newspapers on street corners and spent time in the same caddie yard as Nelson. Their insecurity is understandable; they knew how tough life could be for them if they failed to produce on the course. There were fewer options if they didn't succeed at golf, because most of them didn't have a college education to fall back on, as is the case with today's generation of tour golfers.

Thus, their fear of failure drove them to positive accomplishments. In many ways, a secure tour player is a foolish tour player. If you aren't improving and moving forward, you are falling behind because others are improving. You can't stand still and maintain your place on today's tour. Accordingly, security for a tour player has to be found outside his golfing accomplishments. Family, friends, and religion have seemed to offer the most security to tour players over time. These things offer security to the players that they cannot find on the course.

Fear of failure can be a positive factor for achievement if a player adjusts to it in the right ways. Jack Nicklaus, who has responded as well as any golfer ever has in pressure situations, has acknowledged feeling fear on the course. "When fear starts to hit me," Nicklaus once said, "my best chance of overcoming it lies in facing it squarely and examining it rationally. Here's what I tell myself: Okay, what are you frightened of? You've obviously played well or you wouldn't be here. Well, go ahead and enjoy yourself. Play each shot one at a time and meet the challenge."

But fear of failure also can have a paralyzing effect if responded to in the wrong ways. Over the past several years I have seen this played out in the PGA Tour Qualifying School. Witnessing the tour hopefuls play the final hole of the six-round marathon, the fear on their faces is so palpable that even the most naive observer can clearly discern it.

Fear of failure to get or keep a tour card can cause some of the ugliest shots imaginable. The fearful player's thinking goes something like this: "I get only one chance a year. What if I don't make it? Can I get a sponsor for next year to play the minitour events? What will my relatives, friends, and peers think of me? Should I just give up on my dream? What if I bogey the next hole?" All of these kinds of thoughts are going through tour-level golfers' minds as they play their last few holes in the qualifying school. Fear of failure creates tension, which causes muscle tightness. This tightness in turn can bring about a lack of rhythm, timing, and tempo, culminating in bad shots. The result is a failure to qualify. Next comes a self-fulfilling prophecy, such as, "There, I told you so. I'm not good enough to be out there on the tour." This fear has derailed hundreds of players as they have made multiple attempts to qualify for the tour.

While fear of failure is relatively obvious to the eye, fear of success is not so easy for the golfer to discover and deal with. Fear of success occurs on a more subconscious level than does fear of failure. Many young tour players have a difficult time winning their first tour event. Their swing instructors have a hard time understanding this, since they can't see any appreciable difference in the player's swings in the closing stages of a tournament in which he shoots a bad score. They refer the golfer to a sports psychologist, and after exploring many possible reasons for failure, the golfer frequently brings up the fear of success. The golfer admits that if he wins, people will then expect him to win again and again. This creates pressure that many players don't want anything to do with.

How many times does the leading money winner repeat on any of the professional tours? Part of this failure is the result of the law of averages—since there are so many capable players on tour—but it is also the result of pressure and expectations faced by the defending money leader. Fear of success creates an anticipation of future negative outcomes, which can prevent the player from even achieving a current goal.

During the 1991 PGA Tour season, Corey Pavin was the leading money winner for almost the entire year. The pressures of fear of success and its attendant expectations occurred for Corey from time to time, and we discussed this topic frankly. He fought through the potential negative aspects and won the money title and also was named player of the year by the PGA of America. He was mentally tough enough to turn his fear into a positive challenge. He learned a lot about himself in the process, as does anyone, in any endeavor, who has fear, acknowledges it, and conquers it. It's a great feeling of accomplishment.

Another type of fear that is frequently expressed by golfers of varying abilities is the fear of looking foolish in front of their peers or in front of an audience. For newcomers to golf, there is a very real fear of whiffing the ball.

For talented tour players, I've found that their most consistent fear is related to missing a short putt or a simple pitch or chip shot. In fact, Sam Snead has been quoted as saying, "I shot a wild elephant in Africa thirty yards from me, and it didn't hit the ground until it was right at my feet. I wasn't a bit scared, but a four-foot putt scares me to death."

When I probe for the reasons behind this almost universal fear, what emerges is that a short putt is so simple that even their grandmothers can make it, and if they, the tour players, miss it, they will feel foolish. In fact, I've encountered the phenomenon of the pitching/chipping yips almost exclusively among very skilled players. They put so much pressure on themselves to make these seemingly simple strokes that they create great internal pressure.

One very well known tour player developed the pitching yips to such an extent that he literally felt like he couldn't hit the green with a pitching club from forty feet away. He started putting all such shots rather than risk yipping them, and since he was such a great player, all the analysts and observers thought he was employing some fabulous strategic insight by using the Texas wedge even in some unorthodox situations. He eventually recovered from his case of the yips and went back to using his wedges and pitching clubs, with few people ever aware of his problem.

I can personally relate to the fear of looking foolish in front of people. The first time I ever played golf with Jack Nicklaus was at Pinehurst, North Carolina, and I could have sworn that many hundreds of interested spectators had followed us around the course. Afterward, a friend told me that there could have been no more than seventy-five people in the gallery. But my mouth was dry regardless of how much water I consumed, and it took several holes to establish any type of tempo and rhythm in my swing. And this was after I had played in some pro-ams and worked with a number of well-known tour players.

Check out the eyes of the amateur participants on the first tee of a pro-am. You can see the fear, even in powerful business executives who make million-dollar deals without a flinch. Out of their element, they have a real fear of looking foolish. In fact, for some pro-am participants who get to play as a perk from their company, it's hard to see the outing as the reward it's intended to be, because the golfers are so nervous and worried about failure.

A last aspect of fear concerns another group of golfers. These players have a fear that their best effort is not good enough to achieve the level of play that their self-esteem demands. Therefore, they never "really try." They don't practice, don't take lessons, and don't play the game strictly by the rules. They maintain the charade that they could be really good if they tried hard enough, but they don't have the time or the interest to do so. Their philosophy is "If you don't really try, then you can't fail."

To the contrary, I believe this is the greatest of all failures. Regardless of your ability level, if you don't put forth the effort, you have failed more than if you have tried and not succeeded.

The productive approach to fear on the golf course was aptly handled in a 1987 book by Dr. Susan Jeffers. The book wasn't about golf, but its title could be the perfect slogan if you're dealing with fear in your golf game. Her book was called *Feel the Fear and Do It Anyway.*

GOOD ANGER, BAD ANGER, AND HOW TO TELL THE DIFFERENCE

If you're the kind of golfer who's been known to slam a club into the turf in disgust, throw one up into a tree, or even snap a shaft over your knee, you might well have thumbed to this part of the book before reading any other. If your temper flares red-hot on the golf course, you're probably searching for ways to tame it—or at least channel it more productively. You may be trying to change your ways because you see your temper hurting your score, or because your playing companions see your temper hurting their enjoyment.

The fact is, anger by itself is not necessarily good or bad. It depends on how you channel it or use it. It's up to you to learn to use it positively instead of letting your temper get the better of you. For most golfers, anger is a fact of their games, and the sooner you come to understand it, the better off you—and your playing companions—will be.

The emotion of anger pervades golf more than any other sport, partly because of the long time between shots. In no other sport does an athlete have so much of a lull in the action to allow his temper to boil over. (A few volatile tennis players may disagree.) Indeed, golfers get very emotional over a poorly struck shot or a bad decision in course strategy or club selection. Many times, this emotion is channeled into negative self-evaluation and self-talk, which in turn has a detrimental effect on the rest of the round.

One way to handle the problem is to avoid getting angry. When Bobby Locke came to the United States from South Africa, many observers were amazed at how calmly he accepted his own poor shots and how serenely he dealt with unlucky bounces, bad lies, bumpy greens, and the like. Locke was described as having a demeanor of "benign imperturbability" and some credited his considerable success to his calm deportment.

Most champion golfers, however, have chosen to handle temper in the manner of Sam Snead, who suggested that he played his best golf when in a mental state he called "cool mad." Snead believed that he could most nearly bring his total powers of concentration into use when he was aroused just enough to be a bit agitated but not so much that he lost his cool. This, to me, is the key to understanding anger in golf. All golfers are going to have events on the course—especially on the greens—that will cause anger. Very few people can approach the game as Locke did. Trying to hold in their anger will only result in a big blowup when it finally is released.

The important point to remember is to learn to use the arousal aspect of anger to sharpen your focus and work harder at hitting good shots, while staying cool enough to maintain a game plan in regard to course strategy and management. I work with one tour player who has the unique problem of not being able to get to an optimum level of arousal when he's playing. His personality is such that he has great difficulty in becoming emotionally aroused on or off the course. This lack of arousal has quite probably inhibited his competitiveness on the tour, and in fact he has had difficulty keeping his tour card despite a sound golf swing. He has had some success in trying to use anger as a source of arousal to help his game.

In other sports, it's fairly common to use anger to increase an athlete's arousal level in order to enhance performance. Basketball coaches, for instance, will deliberately act up to receive a technical foul call when their team is playing sluggishly or without full concentration. The technical foul can result in the team becoming angry at the official and thus becoming more aroused and playing harder.

Johnny Miller once compared the arousal level to a tachometer on a sports car. This instrument measures the RPMs of the motor and has a red line, or other indicator, to show when the car engine is revving too fast for its capacity. As a golfer, you want to perform with an arousal level as close to the red line as indicated by your own internal tachometer. Some golfers, like the tour pro mentioned earlier, may have to work extremely hard to get their arousal level up near the red line. Others will have to work equally hard to keep their mental RPMs under the red line. Each golfer has to understand his temperament before he can learn to manage it.

What all golfers can do is learn to use anger in the proper manner. The first step is to learn what anger does to you physically. When people become angry, hormones are released into the bloodstream which cause, among other things, the muscles to tighten and contract. This prepares us to hit out at the source of our anger, which may work well if you're preparing to get into a fistfight with someone, but it's most undesirable for golf. Tight muscles make an effective golf swing nearly impossible to achieve. Therefore, when you feel a surge of anger—such as the feeling which comes over your body after you've missed a short putt—learn to monitor your body. Relax your jaw muscles and the muscles along your neck, back, and shoulders. Take a deep, cleansing breath, which should further relax those muscles tightened by temper.

I encourage athletes with whom I work to do relaxation and breathing exercises off the course, field, or court so that they can learn to understand the difference between the appropriate level of arousal and tension. Learning to monitor and control your tension level not only will help you on the golf course but will also enhance your performance in business. It may also add years to your life if you are prone to any of the physical disabilities related to stress.

An important aspect in controlling the negative side of anger is to determine whether your anger is predominantly inner- or outer-directed. One of the first things I want to know when I begin working with any golfer is whether, when angry, he becomes mad with himself or with other people or outside events. Obviously, everyone is at times angry at all those things, but people do have a tendency toward either inner-placed anger or outer-placed anger.

It's my preference that golfers, while on the course, direct their anger externally rather than internally. Golfers who direct their anger at themselves don't diffuse their anger as effectively as those who direct their anger outwardly. When anger is turned inward and results in extreme self-blame, the effect is virtually always negative.

For example, a player who hits a shot which is ten yards short of the green and in a sand bunker can tell himself how stupid he was for choosing to hit with the wrong club and how he is headed for a deserved score of bogey or worse. Or he can direct his anger outwardly and blame his caddie for the poor club selection. The caddie becomes a socially acceptable lightning rod to allow the player to discharge his anger and keep his internal tachometer below the red line. The player who keeps his anger inwardly directed often fails to develop effective ways to dissipate the tension, and this has a negative effect on his game.

You don't have to use a caddie in order to find a socially acceptable lightning rod to ground your anger before it burns up your scores. I work with one tour player who has to stop and untie and retie his shoelaces after making any score above a bogey. This slight pause between the green and the next tee serves as his lightning rod. With this simple method, he defuses his anger and he arrives on the next tee focused on hitting a good tee shot rather than on the mistakes that caused him to make a bad score and get mad on the previous hole. He stays cool mad, instead of getting hot.

If the greens at your course aren't Augusta National–smooth, you might use the poor work of the greenskeepers as your lightning rod. You also could get mad at the set of clubs you are using. Remember, though, that your lightning rod should only serve a temporary function to reduce excessive anger to a more tolerable level. Don't use it as a continuing crutch to explain poor performances.

CHAPTER SUMMARY

- While golf poses little physical risk to its participants, psychological fear is very real.
- Recognize what specific fear is troubling you. Are you afraid of failure, success, or looking foolish in front of people?
- Understand that anger, in itself, is neither bad nor good. It depends on how you channel your temper.
- Figure out how you direct your anger. Attempt to direct it externally while you're on the course by choosing a socially acceptable lightning rod.

CHAPTER 10

MAXIMIZING YOUR PERSONAL DISTANCE: THE MENTAL SIDE OF THE LONG BALL

Until your game reaches the low-handicap level—and sometimes even once it does—you may share with many of your fellow golfers a fascination and obsession with hitting the golf ball as far as you possibly can. The lure of the long ball is, indeed, as old as the game itself. It's just that today's technological advances in golf equipment make the long ball that much longer—so long, in fact, that when utilized by the game's best players, some established, revered courses are nearly rendered obsolete.

Yet hitting the ball a long way is, and always has been, a matter of personality as much as anything else. And if you understand how your personality works, you can use this knowledge to help you maximize your personal distance.

Shortly before his untimely death late in 1988, I had an opportunity to talk with Davis Love, Jr., about some of the techniques he had used to encourage his son, Davis Love III, to hit the ball long. At that time, the younger Love was one of the longest hitters on the PGA Tour and had been awesomely long when I watched him play during his collegiate career at the University of North Carolina.

During our conversation, Love—the father and teacher—
told me that he had observed an interesting phenomenon
in regard to personality and long hitters in golf. He said
that if you visited a golfer's home and noticed that all the
patio furniture was neatly arranged and that all the shirts
and slacks and so on were similarly organized in the
closet, you knew you were visiting the home of a short
hitter.

In the years since that conversation, I've often thought
of Davis's words. He had been a student of Harvey Penick,
the veteran Texas golf instructor, and both men often
taught by using parables or other types of analogies. I
have only recently come to understand what Davis Love,
Jr., was saying: in order to really move the ball great
distances off the tee, you must be able to make an uninhibited, free-flowing swing with great clubhead speed. Some
golfers have a temperament which perfectly matches this
description of the swing—they are very natural people
who live their lives in a free-flowing, uninhibited fashion.
They are not bound by constraints of appearances or pro-
priety which circumscribe many people's lives. They live
in the present tense and generally in a nonjudgmental
style of life.

Even the nicknames of long hitters connote this type of
personality—"Boom Boom," "Long John," and "Big
Cat." These names conjure up visions of strength and
the devil-be-damned type of swings. The big hitters are
swashbucklers like the pirates of yesteryear. They don't
tiptoe through their swings. They grip it and rip it. Long
hitters tend to be more right-brained, feel-oriented golfers
instead of mechanical players. This is not to say that they
don't have good mechanics or swing technique, but their

primary focus is on *feeling* their swings rather than *analyzing* them.

Fred Couples, the 1992 Masters champion, once shared a story which illustrates how important the mental feel is to a long hitter. Fred never had been able to find a 3-wood which looked good to him when he addressed the ball. But while visiting with fellow tour player Tom Watson during the summer of 1991, he picked up just such a club from the trunk of Watson's car. The club was an experimental prototype and had no markings or shaft bands to denote the stiffness of the shaft. The club felt very good to Couples, and he got permission to try the club in his next tournament.

For several weeks, Couples said he hit some of the best 3-wood shots he had hit in his life. He won a tournament and finished well in several others. Finally the grip on the club became worn and he cut off the old grip to replace it with a new one. On the shaft under the grip, Couples saw an S-200, denoting the shaft stiffness. This amount of flexibility should be too flexible for a person who generates the kind of clubhead speed that Fred does. Once he saw it was an S-200 flex, Couples began hitting the ball poorly with the club, despite his earlier success with it. He just didn't feel like he could hit a club well that had such a whippy shaft in it. Since that time, however, Couples replaced the shaft with a stiffer model and has continued to play well with it, as evidenced by his Masters victory and other successes.

As the Couples anecdote suggests, every golf shot begins in the mind. This is especially true in regard to swings that produce maximum distance. If, in our mental approach to life, we tend to favor a controlled, perfectionistic life-style, it will be hard for us to generate maximum distance on the course.

Overcontrolling golfers are so concerned by mishits that their whole swing is affected by this fear. In his book *You Can Hit the Golf Ball Farther*, Evan "Big Cat" Williams, one of the early long-drive champions, spoke to this point when he said, "If he gets upset by them [mishits] and decides he doesn't want to spray his shots around anymore, he'll start thinking of putting the club on the ball instead of swinging the club. At first, it may look like he's getting somewhere, because he probably will hit more shots straight. But he won't be generating as much clubhead speed that way, so the shots won't travel as far. In time, this woeful lack of distance will begin to gnaw at him, so he'll tap his reserves of brute force and become a slasher. Now, he's not only short, he's back to spraying his shots again."

Williams's conceptual comparison—putting the club on the ball rather than swinging the club—is wonderfully accurate. In order to hit the ball long, you must give up conscious, voluntary control of your club at some point in the swing. You have to let go of control and risk that your swing may not perfectly connect all the dots that swing teachers have determined constitute the perfect swing. But for perfectionists, who hate to feel that they are out of control, this is easier said than done.

In working with my students, I often ask them whether they like to ride high-speed roller coasters or the tilt-a-whirl style rides at amusement parks. Most perfectionists don't like these rides, because they have a sense of being out of control. Most long hitters, though, love them, because they like to live on the edge of the control/out of control continuum.

Many golfers find that they hit the ball farther on the practice tee than they do on the course. This is largely due to the fact that they don't feel they have to control the ball as much on the practice tee as on the course. On the range, you don't have to even look for the balls that you may hit crooked; on the course, it's your ball that you're playing and your scorecard that's suffering the consequences. Therefore, your swing tightens when you step on the first tee. This is especially true for less-experienced golfers, who limit their motion in the back-swing, reduce their coil, and slap at the ball with their hands. They seem to believe that the less movement you produce, the less risk there is of making a mistake in the swing.

Even experienced and talented golfers can fall prey to this way of thinking, particularly on tight courses or in major championships. Their long, powerful swings tighten to the point of mirroring Doug Sanders's swing-in-a-phone-booth action. Contrary to our beliefs, however, shortening the swing doesn't necessarily increase accuracy, but it certainly does decrease distance. If you shorten your swing, you frequently get out of sync in terms of rhythm and timing and often hit the ball more off-line than if you had used your normal swing. Sam Snead once said that he liked long, narrow courses because they tended to make everyone else cut down on their turns while he made his bigger. He said that his swing cue in those circumstances was to "turn and burn."

Snead's phrase illustrates that it is important how to cue

up our distance swings. Bobby Jones used "free wheeling" when he wanted to let out the shaft a bit more on his drives. John Daly used "kill" when he was winning the 1991 PGA Championship. Other players say "grip and rip" when they're seeking to achieve maximum distance. You need to find cue words that are right for you to use when you're attempting to hit the ball long. Try at all costs to avoid phrases that tend to tighten your muscles—tight muscles produce short shots. Instead of saying, "Hit it hard," think, "I want to feel silky or oily on this swing." A silky, oily swing produces more clubhead speed than a hard swing. (If you've ever had a chance to observe golfers trying their hand on one of the electronic swing analyzers that measure clubhead speed, you've seen this proven.)

This is not to suggest that you don't swing the clubhead fast to produce distance. You certainly do, as evidenced by stop-action photographs of tour players at impact. Their clubheads are going so fast from centrifugal force that their faces are extremely contorted. Many amateur golfers, though, confuse hard with fast. There is a huge difference.

In some ways, it is better to think of optimizing your distance rather than maximizing it. By this distinction, I mean that you need to find the maximum distance that you can hit each shot and still maintain reasonable accuracy. This is your optimum distance, keeping in mind that golf is a game of distance and direction, and as the old saying goes, "You have to play your foul balls."

Davis Love III, who won the Players Championship early in 1992 and has become a tour standout, discovered this balance of distance and direction and his game has improved tremendously as a result. While he has fallen out of the top three in driving distance, he has risen significantly in money earnings and, as his Players Championship victory proves, he can win an important tournament. Love III is still one of the longest hitters among those golfers who are among the best on tour, but he controls his shots much better than when he was younger, proof that he has achieved the balancing act necessary for success. If John Daly is to become the best golfer he can be, he will also have to face this balancing act fairly soon.

Most tour players swing at about 85 percent of maximum effort on their tee shots in normal situations. This gives them their optimum distance. On some par-5 holes, however, they may decide that the risk-reward ratio of reaching the green in two shots is favorable enough that they swing at 100 percent of their effort. Curiously, though, these full-bore efforts often don't produce as much distance as their 85 percent swings because trying harder interferes with a free swing, thus reducing clubhead speed as well as producing off-center hits.

You have probably seen the same result of trying harder versus effortless effort when faced with a layup situation on a hole with water in front of the green. You know you aren't going for the green, so your layup swing is effortless and the ball flies farther than your normal shot (sometimes, to your dismay, even into the water that you're trying to avoid). This type of effortless effort is what you want for your optimum-distance swing.

My son once asked me why young children could not draw well. Was it because they lacked the coordination and fine-motor skills? I explained that this was only part of the problem; the young child also lacks the concepts of perspective and proportionality that are so critical to good artwork. This lack of a cognitive understanding of drawing is as much a problem as their lack of physical skills.

Similarly, golfers often lack a cognitive perspective of what a powerful, distance-producing swing looks like and feels like. Percy Boomer, the great British teacher, stressed that a golfer's swing can never be any better than his concept of what a swing should be. Likewise, a person's swing is no more powerful than his concept of what a powerful swing is, or should be. For high-handicap and beginning players, this is a most important area, because they often lack an accurate mental concept of a distance-producing swing. They have never experienced the feeling of the centrifugal force of the swinging clubhead. Ernest Jones used to teach this mental concept of the golf swing by tying a pocketknife to one end of a handkerchief that he had rolled into a ropelike shape. As his students swung the pocketknife on the handkerchief, they felt for the first time the pulling motion of centrifugal force that the clubhead (knife) exhibited.

Too many novice golfers have an erroneous concept of the swing, therefore limiting the distance they can achieve. Some golfers see the swing as a sweeping motion, others a lifting motion, while others perceive it as a chop or scoop. Wally Armstrong, a former tour player turned teacher, uses a variety of teaching aids such as Hula-Hoops, hinging clubs, and the like to get his students to form an appropriate concept of the swing.

I stumbled into an interesting visualization of this concept when, as a young boy, my friends and I cut down some extremely flexible bamboo shoots about eight feet long and stuck some small hedgeapples on the ends of the poles. We then whirled our bodies and the poles and slung the hedgeapples amazingly long distances by creating centrifugal force. Today, anytime I want to feel this force in my golf swing, I mentally re-create the bamboo pole days of my youth. If you have a background as an ice skater, you may remember creating this force by bringing your hands and arms in close to your body and twirling rapidly around a central axis. Use these mental concepts of twirling, slinging, or flinging that you may have learned in other activities and positively transfer them to your golf swing.

A very specific and highly unfortunate example of where a golfer's mental concept of a distance swing affects his performance occurs in older golfers. As we reach our senior years, we often docilely accept the pronouncements of others that loss of distance is inevitable. This is a particular problem for other-directed people—those individuals who don't think for themselves and who passively accept the conventional wisdom of other people. I advocate that you do not go gently into that good night. Fight back against the ravages of the aging process. Keep exercising and doing flexibility training. Swing a weighted club or pipe to stretch those golf muscles.

Dr. Gary Wiren, former director of learning and research for the PGA of America, is now in his mid-fifties and still hits the ball more than 300 yards on occasion. He has done this by maintaining a consistent exercise routine despite traveling around the world teaching and doing research on golf. Barring major health problems, Wiren still will be hitting it 250 yards off the tee when he is in his seventies. Remember, you don't quit exercising because you get old; you get old because you quit exercising.

Your physical strength and fitness are important in producing distance in your swing. So, too, are your swing mechanics. But every golf shot starts in your mind, and for the distance-producing swing, your mental outlook can make or break your results.

CHAPTER SUMMARY

- Hitting the ball a long way is a result of psychological as well as physical factors.
- Most long hitters are more feel-oriented golfers who aren't heavy on swing analysis or self-evaluation.
- Learn to optimize your personal distance by figuring out how far you can hit the ball and still maintain reasonable accuracy. For tour pros, this is about 85 percent of effort.
- Develop an appropriate mental concept of the swing. Learn the difference between swinging hard and swinging fast.

SUCCESSFUL
SELF-TALK

I t seems as if all athletes maintain a running dialogue in their heads as they play their particular sport, but golfers claim the crown in this competition. The nature of golf allows, and to some extent even demands, a great deal of self-talk—whether positive or negative—during the course of a round.

Golfers talk to themselves for two reasons. The first reason we call regulatory. There is a large amount of time between shots. In a round lasting about four hours, it's unlikely that more than one hour is actually spent choosing clubs, lining up shots, and hitting them. Golfers do talk about nongolf matters, of course, but they often use self-talk to get back—or try, anyway—to concentrating on the game. Self-talk can control a golfer's focus. It can also help regulate his emotions and moods. After you miss a short par putt and you start to feel fire creeping up the back of your neck, you might say, "Forget about that putt. Let's hit a good tee shot now. Go through your preshot routine and put a smooth swing on it."

The second reason for self-talk is instruction. Think about how much of your self-talk is concerned with the appropriate skills required to hit a particular shot. This sort of self-talk isn't unique to golf, of course; people often do it when learning such tasks as typing, playing a musical instrument, or driving a car with a manual transmission. When my oldest daughter was learning to drive a car with a stick shift, she would talk aloud as she tried to change gears smoothly. She had no idea that others could hear her. Some golfers do the same thing, and it's not a bad idea. Research suggests that verbal prompts are most effective during the initial learning of a psychomotor skill and at those times when a previously learned skill might interfere with the skill you're currently trying to acquire.

Unfortunately, many golfers know a great deal about negative self-talk and not enough about constructive self-talk that could help them. They're a lot like a young woman who asked me for some advice a couple of years ago as she continued to struggle to earn her LPGA playing privileges. Her swing was sound, but her self-talk was so negative that she never scored as well as she could have.

I suggested that she take two weeks off and caddie for one of her friends who already was on the tour. When the two weeks were up, I asked her what she'd said to her friend when she hit a shot into a bunker. "I told her not to worry," she replied. "Focus on getting the ball up and down from the bunker. You're a good sand player; you can do it."

Then I asked her what she usually said to herself in the same situation. "What a stupid shot!" was her answer. "Can't you hit a green? Now you'll probably make a bogey or worse, and there goes the round." Upon finishing her words, she started to laugh, realizing that in those two short weeks of saying the right, positive things to her friend, she finally had learned how destructive her own self-talk had been to her game. When the next LPGA qualifying tournament came around, she earned her playing card.

That player's lesson is a good one for the many golfers who bad-mouth themselves when they could be giving plenty of self-encouragement. It is stunning how negative golfers can be with themselves, whether the words are spoken aloud or internalized.

A good approach is to imagine that the ball that you've just sliced into the trees isn't yours but belongs to someone else. Think how you would talk to that golfer if you were caddying for him. Undoubtedly, you would find some kind words to say—you wouldn't berate him. Nor should you berate yourself with self-talk. Admittedly, with the demise of caddies, most golfers play in a cart these days and there is no one around to offer encouraging words. You have to provide your own constructive self-talk, keeping in mind that it does no good to brood very long over one poorly executed shot. Use some humor if that's your style. You might have duck-hooked the ugliest drive imaginable into the depths of the forest, but you might have stayed out of the poison ivy. There is something positive to be said about most situations.

The talented tour player Chip Beck, who tied the all-time PGA Tour scoring record with a 59 in 1991, is wonderful at seeing the bright side of things, and this contributes to his success. "I really play well with Chip," fellow tour player Ted Schulz told *Golf Digest* in a 1992 article about Beck. "His self-talk is just so positive, it rubs off on you. He can hit a really horrible shot and afterward talk so well to himself."

Keeping things positive is at the top of the list when it

comes to making your self-talk as effective as possible. But it is only one of six things you can do. These strategies can help you talk yourself into success instead of trouble when the game, as it too often can, leaves you talking to yourself.

SIX WAYS TO IMPROVE YOUR SELF-TALK

1. Keep things positive. Most average golfers are much too tough on themselves on the course. They chide themselves after bad shots and seldom talk positively. This is in contrast to their behavior on the practice tee, where, unlike tour golfers, they take it easy on themselves. The opposite should be true: work yourself hard on the practice tee, but be your own best friend on the course, and that includes self-talk that is positive, encouraging, and constructive. Amateurs often display a skewed sense of expectations that compounds their negative self-talk. In working with golfers, I often ask them to grade their shots on a scale of 1 to 10, with 10 being the highest grade. A shot that a tour pro might give an 8 might receive a 5 from an amateur with a lot less talent who ought to be satisfied with it. Negative self-assessments such as these only do harm.

2. Be dispassionate. Whether self-talk is regulatory or instructional, it should be spoken in a matter-of-fact tone. Most golfers simply can't afford to be too high or too low emotionally while they're on the course. Self-talk is most effective when you perceive that you are outside yourself looking in and talking to yourself from this objective perspective rather than being too emotionally involved. This style of self-talk can also serve the regulatory function of helping to calm your nerves in tense situations.

3. Analyze, don't evaluate. Instead of telling yourself how dumb you were after making an error—and using choice names such as idiot, donkey, numbskull, or worse for yourself—try to focus on the reason behind your bad shot. Were you poorly aligned? Did you make a bad swing? Were you trying to hit the wrong kind of shot for the situation? Or a shot that was beyond your ability level? Cool analysis will help you avoid repeating the mistake.

Some of the game's best players, such as Tom Kite and Gary Player, will take practice swings just *after* they've hit a bad shot in an attempt to analyze why they mishit and rehearse the swing they're planning to use on the next stroke. I suggest that after hitting a bad tee shot, for instance, you should analyze why you struck the shot the way that you did, but by the time you leave the teeing ground you should have begun to focus on the next shot facing you. This analytical self-talk is much more functional than heaping negative self-evaluative statements on yourself.

4. Temporarily defend your ego. This may seem to be a strange function of self-talk. After all, why should you waste your self-talk time defending your ego? The answer is simple: golf, like life, is too difficult a game both physically and mentally to play without protecting your ego. Even the greatest champions have rationalized temporarily about weather conditions or bumpy greens. They just can't believe their ball broke away from the hole. It just can't be a faulty stroke, it must be an imperfection in the green (even if the golfer was also the course designer).

There is a caveat, however. It's important to note that

the use of ego defense mechanisms in self-talk should be only for a temporary purpose on the course. Don't repeatedly deny reality. Blame the poor putting surfaces while you're playing—and putting poorly—but head to a smooth practice green when you've finished your round to determine the real cause of your problems. It may have been the greens, or it may have been your stroke, and you need to find out the truth.

5. Talk in the present tense. Instead of telling yourself what has already happened or what might happen, as is the tendency with many golfers, focus your self-talk on the present. Talk yourself through the preparation and execution of the shot you're about to play. Then hit the shot, review the result in a rational, nonjudgmental way, and begin to talk yourself through your next shot. You'll be pleasantly surprised at how this form of self-talk will help your concentration.

It doesn't matter if your self-talk is about something good, or something bad. If it's not in the present, it's not going to be helpful to you. If your playing partners start talking about the ridiculous pin placement on the fourteenth hole while you're playing the twelfth hole, redouble your efforts to keep your self-talk in the present. It will help you learn to control yourself instead of being controlled by others.

6. Decide in advance what you're going to say to yourself. Some golfers just cannot seem to control their self-talk, claiming that old habits, bad breaks on the course, or emotions overwhelm their best intentions. When working with such golfers, I suggest making an audiotape of what they want to tell themselves in certain situations. This can be particularly helpful when you haven't played in a while.

To put together such a tape, describe the situations that give you the most difficulty and decide on an appropriate strategy to handle them. Then write a script of what you plan to think and say when the situation occurs, and make a tape following the script. Play the tape when you get up in the morning and before you go to bed at night. Before long, you will have internalized what you want to say when you're actually on the course and in need of some successful self-talk. You'll be a bit like an actor who has learned lines in preparation for a stage performance. You are presetting your appropriate mental response before you ever tee it up.

CHAPTER SUMMARY

- Golf leaves most players talking to themselves on the course, but it's up to you to make self-talk help your game instead of harm it.
- Effective self-talk can control a golfer's focus and regulate his actions. Learn how to make it do both for you.
- Self-talk can also take the form of instruction while on the course.
- Since golf's frustrations tend to cause people to voice negative feelings, stress positive and encouraging words for yourself.
- The most effective self-talk is spoken as if you are outside yourself looking in—in an analytical, dispassionate way.

HANDLING SOME COMMON
MENTAL-SIDE CHALLENGES

While there is nothing better than a game rooted in solid mental-side fundamentals, you need to be ready to handle golf's psychological trouble spots when they arise. These potential pitfalls, which plague golfers of all ability levels, can spoil your fun and raise your score. But if you understand how these problems diminish your game, you will be able to develop strategies to counteract them.

As with many of the mental strategies we've discussed, these potential stumbling blocks to success often are related to errors committed on the physical side of the game. If you are able to control your psychological approach, however, you will be in a much better position to keep your total game under control. Golfers lose as many strokes to faulty thinking as to flawed swing mechanics.

EXPANDING YOUR COMFORT ZONES

As noted in chapter 7, comfort zones are a clear threat to concentration. But they can also be more harmful to your game if you have a range of scores or situations which limit your ability to improve or keep you from expanding your horizons in regard to people with whom you play and the courses where you play.

Scoring comfort zones are a part of the game that every golfer must deal with at one juncture or another. High handicappers, for example, may be comfortable when their scores fall in the 102 to 110 range, while some low handicappers feel at ease if they shoot between 70 and 75. For either type of golfer, comfort zones present psychological barriers that need to be addressed. A 100-shooter may somehow find that day's secret and begin a round with three consecutive pars. Coming onto the fourth green, he may realize that he is out of his scoring comfort zone and say things such as, "I don't play well enough to be even par after three holes." Chances are the player will waste a few shots on the next several holes until his score is at a more familiar and comfortable level. For a skilled player, similar thoughts may develop if he happens to begin the round with three consecutive birdies.

Scoring comfort zones also operate when you first approach a milestone in your golf career. Think back to the first time that you broke 100, 90, 80, or 70. Most players knock on the door a few times before finally breaking new ground in the scoring column. Frequently, a golfer will have a hot day going—relative to his usual game—and come to the sixteenth tee and begin extrapolating his score. Thoughts such as, "If I just par this hole and bogey the next two I'll shoot . . ." are damaging, because late-hole projections cause you to abandon the present tense and play worse, not better.

"One shot at a time" is a cliché, but a meaningful cliché in this case. *The only way most golfers can break through to a new scoring level is to concentrate on one shot at a time.* There is no doubt that when Al Geiberger and Chip Beck each were on the final green shooting their record rounds of 59 that each knew what he was about to score. But they didn't reach that point in their rounds by projecting how they would stand on the eighteenth green.

Scoring comfort zones broaden with time, and usually after a few close calls. This is to be expected, so don't become disappointed if you fail to break through on your first couple of chances to do so. The thermostat of our comfort zone needs to be slowly adjusted. That is, if your goal is to break 80 but you never have scored lower than an 82, be satisfied at first with a round of 81, followed by an 80. Such incremental improvements make breaking the ultimate barrier that much more feasible.

The same strategy works when you're trying to become more comfortable when playing with different—or, more often, better—golfers. The issue of being comfortable with playing companions stretches all the way to the pro tours. The pros ply their trade at the highest level, but they are human beings, not robots, and there definitely are playing companions that are favored and others that aren't. If you think that you're unique in not having enough gumption to ask to play with your club champion, rest assured that many young tour players are very intimidated upon their first pairing with a veteran pro whom they've idolized while growing up.

If you shoot in the 90s and always play with golfers of the same skill level, don't expect to feel comfortable the first time you find yourself paired with the club champ. Try to build up to your big moment by first playing with

SOME COMMON MENTAL-SIDE CHALLENGES

mid-handicap golfers—people who hit some shots like the club champ but some like you, too.

Broadening your playing-companion comfort zone is not unlike learning to speak in front of a small group, then a slightly larger group, and finally to an auditorium packed with people. Each time you experience a bit of success, your comfort zone will grow larger.

One of the problems with being paired with unfamiliar—and, particularly, more skilled—partners is the expectation that your every move will be examined in microscopic fashion. This is an unrealistic fear, because good players tend to concentrate deeply on their own game and will not pay much attention to the swings of their playing companions.

If you're an inexperienced golfer, you also may have a tendency to hurry your shots in order to "get out of the way" of your new partners. Instead of hitting a good shot, though, you may top or scuff your ball and have to take another swing before getting up with the better player's ball. The haste not only takes more time, it lays waste to your score. There are exceptions, of course, but most low-handicappers are courteous and tolerant of their less-talented playing partners as long as they also are courteous and follow established etiquette. Rather than becoming uptight about your pairing, relax and enjoy watching how a good player moves around the course—it can be some of the best instruction you can get. If your new pairing involves a stranger, but not necessarily a better player, remember that golf is a social game and take the time to get to know your new playing companion. To add to your enjoyment, try to remember to play the course, not your companion, and avoid the pitfalls of unrealistic comparisons.

The golf course comfort zone develops because of a growing familiarity with the type of quality of courses that you might play. If you grew up at public courses changing your shoes on a car bumper, you might have trouble when invited to play at a first-class resort or full-service private club.

For most golfers, the ambience of famous courses causes a natural excitement. In fact, you're probably not a real golfer if you sleep well through the night knowing you're going to have the chance to play at Pebble Beach or Pine Valley the next morning. One well-known amateur was so excited about playing in his first North and South Amateur on the Pinehurst No. 2 course that he spent the night before the competition in his car at the junction of the seventh green and eighth tee. Mike Hulbert, a PGA Tour player, has recalled that the first time he visited the well-manicured Muirfield Village Golf Club in Dublin, Ohio, as a college golfer, he was afraid to take a divot because the fairway grass was so immaculate.

A public course player can feel uneasy when going crosstown to play at the country club. The country club golfer may feel uneasy playing at a celebrity resort course while on vacation. Many a first-time Masters participant has stepped onto the first tee of Augusta National and had a tough time dealing with the history and tradition of the course.

To expand your comfort zone on unfamiliar turf, recall the strategies to handle first-tee jitters discussed earlier in the book. Pay special attention to your psychological preround preparation. Arrive at the course well ahead of time so you can adjust to the new surroundings. Your excitement will cause you to speed up, but try to practice as rhythmically and slowly as you can.

Also try to obtain a scorecard of the course before the day you're going to play. Go over each hole, checking the yardage and details of design, if available. Then try to relate the holes to ones on your home course, or another course that you've played well. Most golfers believe that the holes on an unfamiliar layout are longer than they actually are. Relating the holes to ones that you know can help keep you from thinking that you need a career-length drive in order to reach the greens in regulation. Overswinging in search of extra distance is not going to make your foray onto a new course any easier.

Finally, try to get a look at the course before you play. If possible, start at the eighteenth green and walk the course backward, looking for the best approaches to each green. These are usually easier to see from the green than from the tee, since good architects will seduce the golfer into driving into a spot from which the approach to the green is more difficult.

APPLYING A MENTAL TOURNIQUET
WHEN NECESSARY

When your game starts to erode over several holes—when it suddenly sours after a good start—is there any-thing you can do to "stop the bleeding"? Momentum clearly plays a crucial role in golf—for the good and for the bad. Fortunately, however, there are some things you can do when momentum shifts and you can't seem to do anything right.

1. Take a mental timeout. In team sports, coaches have the opportunity to call a timeout when the opposition is on a roll. The coaches usually shift strategy to change the tempo of the game and disrupt the foe's momentum. The timeout itself acts as a change in momentum. As a golfer, you can't call an actual timeout, but you can slow yourself down. If you're riding in a cart, get out of it when you're twenty to thirty yards away from your ball. These extra steps can give you some mental space. If you prefer to play briskly, take care not to play too quickly when the momentum shifts against you. Be sure to execute your preshot routine and talk to yourself slowly. Remember that you can't make up for all your past mistakes with one great shot.

2. Remove tension and find rhythm. When your game begins to deteriorate, your muscles often tense up and a rhythmical swing becomes nearly impossible. I observe the jaw muscles of the pro golfers I work with to determine their tension state. You need to look out for tense muscles in the back, shoulders, and neck. You can't make an effective swing with tense muscles. Try to reduce your tension by walking more slowly between shots or by humming, singing, or whistling softly to yourself. Take some cleansing breaths that emphasize exhaling tension.

3. Focus on a general swing cue. Too often during momentum shifts, the tendency is to resort to a series of Band-Aid—style tips. As a result, unrelated swing thoughts form a jumble in the mind, affording little chance to make good swings. Try to focus instead on a couple of simple swing cues that have proven to work for you in the past.

4. Don't get mad, get smarter. While it's natural to become angry when your game declines, it inhibits your ability to think rationally and analytically—attributes that you have to have in order to diagnose and correct flaws during a round. As noted in chapter 9, learning to deal effectively with anger is crucial.

5. Recall past successes. When your game begins to slip, remember those times when you were in a similar situation but were able to right your game before it sank too deeply. If you know that you've been able to regain momentum in the past, it helps you create the mind-set necessary to do it again.

6. Don't press. The word has two meanings. One is related to doubling your wagers. Many players feel the way to get back on track is to double the bets on the remaining holes—bigger stakes mean better concentration, or so it's believed. For every person that this works for, many more suffer a dramatic decrease in ability. The other meaning is to try for more distance, a common strategy for golfers whose games are in trouble. Trying to hit it farther rarely does any good.

7. Play more conservatively. When you feel your game slipping, don't put extra strain on yourself by trying to pull off very difficult shots. Try to get the ball in play, even it means using a fairway wood or long iron. Go to the fat of the green instead of the pin if the hole is cut perilously close to water. Mentally divide the green into quadrants and then attempt to hit your approach into the quadrant where the hole is cut. Even if you barely manage to put the ball into the quadrant, you're rarely more than twenty-five feet away from the cup. This still leaves you with a birdie possibility and a fair certainty of a two-putt par.

HANDLING PRESSURE SITUATIONS

There may be no greater challenge, nor greater potential satisfaction, than that found in facing a pressure situation and producing the shot that the competitive crucible demands of you. Early in 1992, Corey Pavin was faced with just such a situation as he played the second playoff hole of the Honda Classic against Fred Couples, the hottest player on tour at the time. Having holed an 8-iron for an eagle on the same hole to get himself into the playoff, Pavin was preparing to hit another short iron in the playoff when a spectator let out a shout: "Shank it into the water!" Such a taunt could have been unnerving, but Pavin backed off the ball, managed a smile, dried his grip, restarted his preshot routine, and hit a good shot to within fifteen feet. When he holed his birdie putt after Couples missed his attempt, the tournament was Pavin's.

What if Pavin had let the spectator—and the moment—get to him? Would that have been choking? No doubt it's popular among many observers to cry choke when a player doesn't produce under pressure. In the 1989 major championships, for instance, many people were quick to say that the four players who had the titles within their grasp before losing—Scott Hoch, Tom Kite, Greg Norman, and Mike Reid—all had choked under the pressure of competing for a major. I'm not certain we'll ever know if that was the case. Only the players know what they were thinking at the time and how their thoughts and emotions affected their swings and decision making under the gun.

For most golfers, whether people choke isn't the pressing question. The undeniable truth is that pressure, real or imagined, can affect one's game. Most everyone has learned to deal with a certain amount of pressure in their job. A certain amount of tension actually is desirable, producing an excitement that helps to stave off boredom. Yet pressure in golf can make people very uncomfortable.

In their book *The Mental Game of Baseball*, authors H. A. Dorfman and Karl Kuehl describe how mental and physical factors are affected by pressure. Mentally, messages from our eyes and ears become unclear and distorted; judgment becomes less accurate; we become indecisive; and our thoughts jump from one thing to another. Physically, there is hyperventilation, altered blood flow, general muscle constriction, reduced range of motion, less-fluid movement, and an inability to see clearly. With all these things happening, it's no wonder your golf game may suffer just as a baseball player's might. To handle the pressure, try these five strategies.

1. Remove yourself from the shot, physically and mentally. When you feel pressure, step away and then move into the shot in one fluid motion. This is not unlike a basketball player who waits until the last moment to step to the free-throw line and accept the ball from the referee. Mentally, remove yourself by visualizing yourself away from the course and at the beach or in your favorite room relaxing at home. Or try to visualize another time when you played a successful shot from a similar situation.

2. Breathe. Under pressure, many golfers forget how to breathe properly. They either breathe very shallowly or hold their breath without even realizing it. Learning how to breathe can work wonders for relieving pressure.

3. Put the shot in perspective. Very few shots are as important as we make them out to be. Cary Middlecoff once said, "I always think before an important shot: What is the worst thing that can happen on this shot? I can whiff it, shank it, or hit it out of bounds. But even if one of these bad things happens, I've got a little money in the bank, my wife still loves me, and my dog won't bite me when I come home."

4. Stretch your muscles like a lazy cat. Think of the way a cat stretches when it suns itself on a windowsill. Going through this elaborate, rhythmic stretch not only can relax your muscles, it can relax your mind, too. It can help you feel long and loose, and it can preset the flowing tempo that you want to exaggerate on a pressure shot.

5. Hum or sing to yourself. Depending on the tolerance of your playing partners, you can do this under your breath or out loud. During tense moments of the 1988 World Series, television viewers saw Los Angeles Dodgers pitcher Orel Hershiser sitting alone in the dugout with his eyes closed and his lips moving. Hershiser said later, "I was too excited about being in a World Series and winning. So I relaxed and sang hymns to myself." Former tour player Jerry Heard and current player Fuzzy Zoeller have whistled between shots to ease their tension. You don't have to be musically inclined to do this—you're striving to relax yourself, not entertain someone else.

SOME COMMON MENTAL-SIDE CHALLENGES

HOW TO HOLD ON TO THE LEAD ONCE YOU HAVE IT

Holding on to the lead in golf, whether in match or stroke play, is one of the most psychologically intriguing aspects of the game. But it's not unique to golf. Once, during the broadcast of a preseason pro football game, commentator John Madden noted as a golf leaderboard was flashed during the game that the winner most likely wouldn't come from the eight names listed on the screen. Madden's broadcasting partner wondered aloud what made Madden, a golf neophyte, make such a prediction. "It's easier to chase than be chased," Madden said.

Indeed, that is the case in golf. Often the leader becomes too conservative, changing the game plan that got him into the lead to begin with. The challenger, believing that he has nothing to lose, freewheels his way up the board and catches up. A common complaint among those tour golfers who have had difficulty maintaining a lead is that they begin to "wish" the ball onto the green and into the cup rather than make an authoritative effort to strike good shots. Keeping this in mind, one of the first things you can do to thwart a loss of skills while you're leading is to focus on the process of hitting good shots, regardless of how large your lead may be.

Try to maintain the same swing cues that you used to get yourself in the lead. Don't become overly conscious of one bad shot you might play at a critical point in the match or tournament. In advance of your round, develop a game plan for several eventualities. Imagine, for instance, that you will have a one-up lead going to the seventeenth hole. How will you attempt to play the hole? A strategy conceived in the preround calm is almost always better than one born in the heat of battle.

Another way to prepare yourself in advance is to recognize which is the lowest-numbered iron that you can hit with the greatest precision on a consistent basis. This iron and all the higher-numbered clubs are designated as scoring clubs. The rest are placement clubs. According to one teaching professional who advocates this system, when a player has a scoring club in hand and the pin is in a reasonable position, he has a green light to shoot for the stick. If he must use a placement club, he has to try to play the shot to the fat part of the green. If you're trying to hold on to the lead, you might want to redesignate your scoring clubs. Instead of going for the pin with a 5-iron and higher, change to a 7-iron. But once you've made this decision, remain psychologically aggressive, remembering that becoming overly conservative is a quick way to lose your hard-earned advantage.

DEALING WITH GAMESMANSHIP

Although it's true that mind games, or the little mental "games within the game," were more commonly practiced years ago in golf, they still exist, and you need to be prepared to deal with them. Mind games fit into three general categories: the powers of distraction, intimidation, and suggestion.

Distraction

Distractions come in many forms, ranging from absent-mindedly jingling coins while an opponent hits or allowing your shadow to fall over your opponent's ball all the way to actions bordering on outright cheating. A good friend of mine once had to put up with a regular playing partner who smoked a pipe and always put the pipe down on the ground parallel to his target line before playing a shot. My friend was unnerved because he didn't know whether his companion was deliberately violating the rules. This uncertainty is usually a key element in distracting mind games. It's like a baseball pitcher with a reputation for doctoring the ball before he pitches—whether or not the pitcher is actually breaking the rules, the batter is doomed to have his concentration broken.

You can also be distracted by golfers who seek to disrupt your playing tempo. Paired with a deliberate golfer, they may try to speed up; with a golfer who prefers a quick pace, they may purposely slow down so the foe becomes impatient and begins to rush his shots. One of the most notable examples of rhythm distraction occurred in the playoff for the 1947 U.S. Open between Lew Worsham and Sam Snead. Each faced short putts inside three feet. It appeared that Snead was away, but when he settled over his ball Worsham asked officials for a measurement. Because a tape measure couldn't be found quickly, there was a delay, and after Snead was found to indeed be away by about one inch, the Slammer missed his putt. Worsham then holed his putt to win the championship. Snead never won a U.S. Open.

INTIMIDATION

This type of mind game can—and often does—occur without the conscious knowledge of the intimidator. As mentioned previously, rookies on the pro tours can be awed upon their first pairing with established stars. The rookies become overly conscious of what the veteran will think of their games. In the old days, there probably were more golfers who really did try to intimidate younger golfers by their presence, but that type of golfer is rare today. Thus, intimidation is largely a self-imposed, but still potent, mind game.

SUGGESTION

The power of suggestion comes in various guises, from open and obvious to subtle and crafty. A veteran LPGA player once told me how adept Hall of Famer Louise Suggs was at using the power of suggestion. When faced with a hole with a blind tee shot, Suggs would call out to her caddie across the tee, "Is this the hole where there is water on the left and out of bounds on the right?" The question was voiced just before her playing companions were preparing to play. Was Suggs simply asking an information-seeking question? Perhaps. Were they questions within the rules? Certainly. Was she employing a mind game of suggestion? More than likely.

In the days before golfers referred religiously to specific

yardages before playing their shots, old-timers practiced another form of the power of suggestion involving club selection. Since peeking into a bag to gauge your partner's club selection is within the rules, veteran pros would try to deceive their fellow golfers by having the head covers switched on their 3- and 4-woods. The veterans also would take a longer club on par-3 holes but make a much softer swing. When the rookies would pick the same club and employ a full swing, their shots would airmail the green.

All three forms of mind games have one common denominator: no one can play mind games with you unless you give them permission. If you learn to control your mind, the actions of others won't affect you.

WHEN THE PUTTING BLUES GET YOU DOWN

You haven't gotten any swing instruction in this book, and you're not going to get any mechanical advice now on putting, but this aspect of golf is so bedeviling for so many golfers that it warrants discussion from a mental point of view. Putting is different from the rest of golf: you roll the ball along the ground instead of fly it through the air. It appears to take little physical strength. Little children and octogenarians can experience putting success. You can grip the putter in many different ways and still find the hole.

Putting is so distinct from the rest of golf that some players have argued that a putt shouldn't count as a full stroke. Ben Hogan and Dave Hill are two such advocates, both of whom suffered from the demons that afflict even the very best players on the greens. Making the hole larger than its current 4¼-inch diameter has been proposed in order to neutralize putting skill. In the 1930s, on the suggestion of Gene Sarazen, a larger hole was tried in an experiment, but it didn't prove to make much difference.

Almost no one will admit to being a good putter—it's as if doing so makes you less honorable than the next golfer, who earns his score with a solid tee-to-green game. Some think that bragging about their putting will anger the golf gods. They see it like bragging about how many miles they've gotten on a set of tires, then having two flats in a week's time.

Poor putting is damaging not only in itself, but in the deleterious domino effect it can exert on the rest of your game. To make up for missed putts, it's common to put more pressure on your full-swing game. In trying to get shots close enough to the hole so you won't have to worry about the putts, your full shots usually deteriorate rapidly.

To handle putting problems more maturely, you must come to grips with two things: the concept of finality in putting, and the existence of fate, chance, or luck involved with every stroke on every green, with every type of golfer.

Putts are the last stop on the bus route. Nerves start to interfere with putting long before they affect other strokes because you know that once a putt is missed, there is no way to redeem yourself—the blot already is on the scorecard. Recovery options exist from tee to green, but not on the putting surface. For all golfers, regardless of their skill level on other shots, there is the expectation to make the first putt on a green. The "what ifs" often develop, from the anticipation of making a birdie putt to the dread of what if you miss the par putt, or bogey putt, or . . .

The worst case of finality I've seen on the greens belonged to a low-handicap orthopedic surgeon who was having big trouble with his putting. He would freeze over his putts and struggle, truly struggle, to get the putterhead started away from the ball. I asked him what he thought about just before beginning his takeaway, and his response was memorable. "Suicide," said the poor-putting doctor.

One way to ease your tensions on the greens is to recognize the role that luck plays in putting. Researchers have discovered that once a putt becomes longer than twelve feet, chance plays almost as important a role as skill in getting the ball to drop in the hole. Old ball marks, spike indentations, worm castings, and irregularities in the grass have a great deal to do with whether a putt makes or misses. This lack of control over the ball is a big source of consternation for many golfers with putting difficulties.

There is nothing anyone can do about those vagaries of the greens, but you can make the effort to put yourself in the best physical and psychological position to make the best stroke you have on each putt. You cannot control the ball all the way to the hole, but you can control your mental condition when you make your stroke. Execute a consistent preputt routine, try to remain positive, and, by all means, if your putts are finding the hole, be proud of your accomplishments.

KEEPING SLOW PLAY FROM DRAGGING YOU DOWN

There can hardly be a golfer in existence these days who hasn't had a round ruined by the effects of a slow pace of play. It seems as if slow play is creeping over the game like a kudzu vine with its annoying, agitating characteristics. I shall leave the solutions to slow play to golf associations and other organizations, but as long as slow play plagues the game, you need to be able to deal with it so it doesn't drag your game down.

Most golfers say they don't like to play slowly, and they admit that slow play hurts their game to some degree. While you can't snap your fingers and eliminate the problem, you can use the following four methods to keep slow play from becoming a noose around your game.

1. Identify the pattern of movement in the players in front of you. Regardless of how slowly they may play, all golfers have a definite pattern of movement. Note which player in the group is likely to replace the flagstick, which one is last to leave the green, and which one lingers at the edge of the putting surface to mark down his score. Determining how the group in front of you moves allows you to develop some sense of rhythm as to when you will be able to hit your next shot. Slow play can wreak havoc on rhythm, and if you don't find ways to create your own rhythm, the herky-jerky nature of slow play will creep into your swing.

2. Disengage your mind from golf and let your thoughts turn to nongolf matters. As discussed in the chapter on concentration, the best approach to golf is to relax your mind between shots—there are times when you want your mind to wander. But when you let your mind temporarily disengage from golf, don't think about tension-producing subjects like a bad stock-market manuever, marital difficulties, or the braces that your children are going to need. Think pleasant thoughts, and be ready to play when the fairway or green is cleared, with a signal that quickly brings you back to focus on golf.

3. Develop a signal to draw your attention completely back to the shot at hand. As detailed in the chapter on preshot routines, this signal is always important, but it truly can be of help if you're caught in a snail's-pace round of golf. Avoid using the time you have between shots to fiddle with various swing cues—this slow-play habit destroys many games. Try to move directly into your shot with the same rhythm as if there were no other golfers on the course. While this is difficult, it's the ultimate slow-play goal.

4. Avoid discussing the negatives of the slow pace with your playing companions. This is important because players often deal effectively with a slow pace until one of their companions starts harping about how much it's hurting his game. This negativity can quickly snowball through an entire foursome. While you can't control the way your playing companions think, you can control your own statements and choose to ignore what the others are saying. Complaining about the problem among yourselves won't help solve it.

CHAPTER SUMMARY

- Expanding your comfort zones in regard to score, playing partners, or courses takes time. Broaden your comfort zones one step at a time.
- When the momentum shifts and "the wheels start to come off" your game, take a mental timeout, focus on a general swing cue, recall past successes, and don't let anger get the best of you.
- Pressure affects even golf's greatest players. No one is immune, but you can recognize what pressure does to you physically and emotionally. Under competitive fire, keep the shot in perspective and try to enjoy the moment.
- To hold on to a lead in either match or stroke play, have an advance plan as to what you're going to do. Remember that you cannot wish the ball into the cup. Keep making authoritative swings.
- Mind games can take the forms of distraction, intimidation, and suggestion. No mind game can have a negative effect on your game, however, unless you allow it.
- To deal with putting problems, remember that a certain amount of luck or fate is involved on all putts regardless of how skilled the putter might be. Get yourself in the best physical and mental condition before you begin your stroke and put your best stroke possible on each putt; that's all you owe yourself.
- Slow play is an unfortunate aspect of the modern game, but you can minimize its negative effects on your game by doing your best to maintain your customary preshot routine and avoid dwelling on the pace and complaining about it to your playing companions.

JUNIOR-SENIOR STRATEGY: STARTING RIGHT AND AGING WELL

Although the instruction within this book is applicable to golfers of all ages, as well as ability levels, the special issues of junior and senior golfers warrant discussion. One of the questions I'm asked most frequently is, "How do I get my child or grandchild interested in playing golf?" Often that question is posed by someone over age fifty—a senior under golf's classification system—who is also curious about how to keep his own game sharp as he ages. In this chapter, we'll address the issues of junior and senior golf, with an eye toward keeping the game enjoyable for both age groups.

STARTING SOMEONE OUT ON THE RIGHT FOOT

The subject of junior golf is of personal interest to me because I have a thirteen-year-old son and because I have shared so many pleasant hours on golf courses with my father. While many of today's parents seem most concerned about how to produce a tour superstar (we'll touch on this matter later), the priority for a parent should be to develop within his child the healthy respect for playing golf as long-term enjoyment. Some children are able to forge a competitive career of some sort, but most young-sters will end up playing the game recreationally. And there is no doubt that someone who learns the game prop-erly as a youth will have the opportunity to enjoy it more as an adult.

For most children, golf appears to be a boring game. There is not a great deal of apparent physical activity as in action-oriented sports such as basketball, football, soccer, or hockey. And in contrast to team sports, where kids compete against their peers in organized leagues, golf often is a solitary endeavor—it can even be lonely at times. The game requires a unique playing space and relatively expensive equipment. Learning golf also can be expensive, but the game needs to be learned early from competent instructors so poor habits don't become in-grained during the early developmental stage. Although bargains exist—through clinics and group lessons—in-struction can be a difficult and expensive thing to come by, depending on where you live.

Acknowledging these negatives, there are six ways for you as parents to try to increase the likelihood that your child will become interested in golf.

1. The concept of readiness to learn must be under-stood. One time I asked Jack Nicklaus, the father of five children, how soon kids should be encouraged to play golf. His answer: "You should start them as soon as they are as interested in golf as they are in chasing bullfrogs." At the time, Michael, his youngest son, was joining the family on some rounds of golf. Michael would hit a few shots, then his attention would turn to a pond where a number of frogs made their home. The rest of the family would continue their golf while Michael chased the frogs. Eventually, Michael rejoined the family and played a few more holes.

Nicklaus is a good example of a parent understanding the concept of readiness. Instead of forcing his youngest child to play golf, Nicklaus permitted him to hit as many shots as he was interested in hitting and then let him move on to other things. Trying to push children faster than their developmental level of readiness allows not only does little good in skill development, but frequently causes them to dislike the very game that you want them to enjoy. You can help your child develop readiness for golf by having him join you for a few holes during a twilight round. Let him hit short shots to the green and putt out on each hole. These shots are more likely to result in success than the longer shots which require adult strength and skills.

2. Allow your child to associate the golf course with pleasant experiences. Quality time spent with parents can be most pleasant for a child. While this means that you may not be able to concentrate fully on your own game—remember, kids are born knowing that the top of the backswing is the best time to make a loud noise—it's important to demonstrate your interest and respect for the game. Point out the beauty of the course and encourage the child to associate golf with nature. While it sounds a bit like a bribe, reward the child for good golf-course etiquette by letting him enjoy a snack in the clubhouse afterward. This positive reinforcement will increase the chances that the child will like his golf experiences. Also allow your child to bring a friend with him occasionally. This will help him to enjoy the golf experience by sharing it with someone his own age.

3. Remember that children have short attention spans. To a small child, a round taking more than four hours can seem like an eternity. Keep in mind that your perception of time, as an adult, is much different from your child's. Take the middle-aged man who has no interest in fishing. He believes it's because the first time his father took him fishing, they spent five hours together on a lake on a hot summer day. The father may have had a grand time, but the son developed a negative reaction to angling that has lasted his entire life. If you have your child with you on the course, let him chip and putt when you reach a green, assuming that you're not holding up other players. But don't expect him to do it on every hole. This doesn't mean that he's not interested, just that his attention span is still short. Nine holes at a time is more than enough for most young children.

4. Always leave the child wanting more. As noted early in the book while discussing why people are attracted to golf, people generally like to return to tasks which they view as unfinished. Golf certainly fits this bill, since it never can be mastered, and with a child you often have to make the determination when he should quit. Suggest that he leave the practice area before his enthusiasm wanes. This may interrupt your practice session, but it's better than leaving your child in the golf boat for five hours, with the possible consequences.

5. Children learn best by imitation. Some adults try to teach their children by using the same verbal methods by which many instructors teach adults. It's much more effective and efficient to let children watch good golfers and learn by imitation. I let my son watch Ben Crenshaw's putting instruction video with the sound turned off because I wanted him to process the rhythm and tempo of Crenshaw's stroke without the technical information more appropriate for adults.

Since there are fewer caddying opportunities available today, most kids must watch their parents in order for observational learning to occur. Pro tournaments on television and specialized videotapes such as Sybervision also are possible tools. Remember that the child should absorb the whole swing instead of technical details. When choosing an instructor for your child, try to find one who specializes in teaching juniors. Some teachers have a personality and method that seem to click with younger golfers, and this can make the learning process more productive and enjoyable for your child.

6. Start with high-success experiences. Many parents start their children with cut-down woods which do little more than frustrate the child, because it's tough for young children to get the ball airborne with a wood—even with the ball teed up. It's better to first give your child an appropriately sized putter and have him start with short putts where he can enjoy a high success rate. From there, the child can attempt long putts and eventually begin chipping. When the young child sees some success with his short game, and as his strength and coordination improve, he can begin hitting lofted clubs with the ball teed up. This combination helps the child get the ball airborne and minimizes the frustration of hitting ground balls.

Some Hints if Your Child Is Interested in Competition

It is both a blessing and burden to have a child who excels at golf. You take pride in his successes and happily anticipate the time when he will play college golf, or even, if all goes well, advance to a career as a professional golfer. On the flip side, however, you worry if he is too serious about golf, or not serious enough. You know that compared to the number of junior golfers who aspire to earn college golf scholarships or have successful pro careers, the available spots are relatively few. You fret about early burnout and bemoan the high cost of paying for your child's golfing efforts.

All are worthwhile hopes and legitimate fears. Unfortunately, there are few easy answers for parents with a child who has a burgeoning competitive career. Each child is an individual with goals, desires, and personality traits all his own. But by all means try to get your child on challenging courses and against appropriate competition if he shows some competitive talent. Don't be under the false belief, though, that your child has to play the bulk of the AJGA (American Junior Golf Association) schedule in order to become a competitively tough player. If you have the financial means and your child the talent and inclination, a national schedule is certainly possible— just don't think it's absolutely necessary.

If your child is good enough to play college golf, help him realize that education should be his first concern. No matter how good a golfer your child may be when he steps on the college campus as a freshman, many variables will affect his competitive path from there. Teenagers can be seduced into thinking that they are sure bets to make it on tour after college, but in reality there are few sure bets and many more collegiate golfers who squander their chance to earn a meaningful education. You don't have to deliver it in an overbearing way, but make the education message very clear to your aspiring golfer. Neither of you will regret it.

ADAPTING FOR SUCCESSFUL SENIOR GOLF

Thanks to the presence of the Senior PGA Tour over the past decade, everyone has had the chance to see that a person's golf skills can remain honed and formidable even after he turns fifty. Indeed, the examples abound— from the consistently fine play of seniors such as Lee Trevino, Jack Nicklaus, and Chi Chi Rodriguez to the achievements of Jerry Barber, who has continued to shoot his age on tour as he reaches age seventy-five. As someone who not too long ago turned fifty myself, these players are an inspiration. And from a professional standpoint, having counseled a number of Senior PGA Tour golfers and several top-ranked senior amateurs, I've gotten a bit of insight into how seniors can maintain their golfing skills.

In working with seniors, I've noticed a direct relationship between the golfers' philosophy of life and their success in senior golf. Many players begin to set limits on themselves simply because they have reached a certain juncture in life. They are labeled as seniors and therefore develop self-fulfilling prophecies about life and about golf. "I'm too old to learn a new shot," they say. Or they pass off problems as a direct result of getting old instead of searching for the real cause. "My putting sure has fallen off in the last year or so—I must be getting old."

Yes, physical limitations do come with the territory of advancing years. To tell yourself otherwise is foolish. In sports medicine, it's a generally accepted principle that from our mid-twenties on we lose approximately 1 percent lean body mass per year of life. This translates directly into a loss of muscular strength. This loss, however, doesn't happen between our forty-ninth and fiftieth birthdays, but is a cumulative effect occurring incrementally over the years. The greatest effects are obviously felt during the senior years. But you don't have to sit idly by and let the strength loss go unchecked.

A well-planned exercise program for muscle tone and flexibility can alleviate some of this loss of strength. A golfer who feels that he is too old to exercise is exhibiting another example of the self-fulfilling prophecy. If he chooses not to exercise, he will become older much faster than his peers who follow a well-designed exercise program. Remember that you don't get too old to exercise— you get old if you don't exercise.

Still, senior golfers have to be prepared to adjust their games. As William Arthur Ward said, "The pessimist complains about the wind; the optimist expects it to change; the realist adjusts the sails." Seniors have to be realistic, willing to explore all avenues of adjustment.

Many problems faced by senior golfers occur on or around the greens. Some claim not to see the roll of the greens as well as they did when they had younger eyes. Other seniors report that their nerves are worn out, and they get the twitches or yips while putting. Sometimes these twitches extend to chips and pitch shots. If you have these problems you might consider following the examples of senior tour players such as Orville Moody, Charles Coody, and Jim Ferree, and switch to one of the long-shafted putters that you wield pendulum-style. While the method employed with the long putter undoubtedly removes some of the small muscles from the stroke, there is a psychological component as well. It's as if the switch from a conventional blade to the more radical putter wipes the slate clean—previous putting failures are erased, and the golfer is free to putt with renewed confidence. This seems to be especially true of Moody, always a superb ball-striker, who went from being an awful putter to a good one when he put the long putter in his bag.

In addition to the long putter, don't forget about other high-tech equipment to give your game a boost. Finding the proper shaft for your strength and swing is critical. Some senior tour players have abandoned traditional balata-covered golf balls in favor of newer designs with harder covers that afford more distance. While there is some adjustment in terms of how the nonbalata ball "feels," particularly around the greens, most of the seniors make the change without much problem.

You may want to consider a two-piece ball, and with the advances in technology you can look for balls constructed in such a way to suit your particular game. If you have trouble getting your driver up in the air, for instance, certain balls are manufactured to provide a higher trajectory. Aside from the tangible rewards from changing equipment, a more important point may be the fact that you are constantly searching for new options and are open to change. This attitude of openness and receptivity to new challenges is a sure indication of a golfer (and a person) who is continuing to grow rather than one who is stagnating and drawing inward.

Despite the drawbacks of growing older, there are some things you can take advantage of. As you grow older and become more mature as a person, you should also become more self-accepting. This can help a great deal on the golf course. It is also easier for many senior golfers to play within the limitations of their games than it is for their younger counterparts. Remember when you were younger and stronger and a certain senior golfer, short and straight and crafty around the greens, took you to the cleaners with regularity? Remember how, in the back of your mind, as you muttered in defeat, you secretly wished your game was a little bit more like the older man's? Well, now it is—you just have to take advantage of it.

CHAPTER SUMMARY

- If you're thinking about getting your child to develop an interest in golf, don't do so until he has an appropriate readiness level.
- Always associate golf with being a pleasant experience, and always make sure your child leaves the course eager to come back again instead of being bored by too much golf. Children have short attention spans.
- If your child has talent and a desire to play competitively, try to provide him with reasonable opportunities, but don't falsely believe that he has to play a full national schedule in order to be successful.
- For senior golfers, it's important to acknowledge the physical limitations of growing older—but don't give in

to them. Exercise regularly to keep your muscles strong and flexible.

• As you grow older, take advantage of the many technological advances in golf equipment to keep your game fresh and potent.

• Don't overlook the positives of aging. You should be wiser in addition to being older. Use your maturity on the golf course. Don't fall victim to negative self-fulfilling prophecies just because you're getting older.

HISTORY, OBSESSION, AND TRAITS OF THE GREATS

None of the instruction herein is going to help your game if you fail to take an honest and realistic look at how you really play. It is very easy in golf to practice self-deception. It is also very damaging. Therefore, try to make a concerted effort at the following three resolutions.

1. Resolve to be totally honest with yourself about your game. Most amateurs, and some professionals, fail to level with themselves as far as their golf games are concerned. This often results from a lack of objective information about their game. Very few players know, for example, how far they consistently hit each club. Many deceive themselves into thinking that the 170 yards they once hit a 6-iron in thin air with a strong tailwind is their average distance with the club. Golfers also confuse carry-and-roll distance with carry-only yardage. Since the design of most American courses dictates approaches that fly onto the green, know how far your shots go through the air.

Also avoid kidding yourself about the predominant flight pattern of your shots. If you hit a low slice 80 percent of the time, it makes little sense to try to attack a certain hole with a high draw. Until you have the skill to actually hit a hook, you're better off allowing for your slice and playing it. If you assess your skills and work to improve the weaknesses, you can avoid fooling yourself into making stupid mistakes. Be honest with yourself. How far do you really hit the ball? How accurate are you with your short irons, the scoring clubs? How good are your approach putts? You should be uncompromisingly honest in answering these questions in order to improve your game.

2. Resolve to have realistic perceptions about your game. Being realistic follows being honest, because you won't understand your limitations until you know your true ability. My golf experiences run the spectrum these days, from rounds with the tour pros whom I counsel, to social golf with friends. Some of my high-handicap friends amaze me with how often they will attempt to pull off shots that the tour pros never would try on their best days. Successful pros have learned to assess realistically the shot ahead of them and match it to the skill level needed to accomplish it. If the only realistic option from a given situation is a chip back to the fairway, they do it. Many amateurs, on the other hand, rarely take their medicine. They attempt heroic recoveries that they have little chance of hitting successfully.

For many golfers, their unrealistic skill assessment comes from watching televised golf. How often do TV announcers proclaim a golfer to be faced with an "impossible" shot with "no chance" of pulling it off? Then the pro hits a very good shot and we're left to wonder what hole the announcer was actually watching. What we—and the announcer—were unable to see was the player's own view of his shot possibilities. He may have seen a way to make the shot with a wide margin of error, therefore creating a much more realistic play than depicted by the announcer.

Distances achieved by tour players also are skewed sometimes on telecasts. We hear that a certain player used an 8-iron on a 175-yard par-3 and are amazed at his strength. But we aren't told that because of tee placement, hole location, and the wind, the player actually has a shot that's playing to 150 yards, making the 8-iron a realistic club selection for the pro.

3. Resolve to know and acknowledge your thinking and playing patterns. Each golfer has systematic and idiosyncratic thinking patterns which affect his play. Take the time to analyze your thought patterns and use your knowledge to your advantage. For example, when you make a birdie, do you immediately lose focus on the next hole and make a bogey or worse? Does missing a short putt rattle your concentration and confidence for a couple of holes? What happens after you hit a shot into the water or out of bounds? Do you proceed calmly, or do you let the setback throw you into a tailspin?

If you play as many as twenty rounds during a season, analyze your specific patterns of play. Beginning with the first hole, divide your round into six sets of three holes each, and determine how you stand in relation to par for each of the six sets. Pros and amateurs alike often have a distinct pattern of good and bad holes. If you find a pattern on your scorecards, you can try to develop ways to retain the good sets while eliminating the poor ones.

Caring About Your Game without Being Obsessed with It

It's fairly easy for some golfers to go overboard in regard to the attention that they pay to golf. More than a few golfers have allowed their zeal for the game to wreck a marriage or diminish their relationship with their children. Even for tour pros who earn their livings playing golf, the game should never be the end-all of their lives. In fact, when I counsel tour pros I stress to them that golf should only be a part of their life; it shouldn't *be* their life. I elaborate by telling them that if all they ever contribute to society is their playing on tour, they've done very little. They are no different from a business executive who immerses himself in a job with no regard for family, friends, or community.

Unfortunately, tour pros and recreational golfers become obsessed with their golf games. It can take someone else—spouse, family member, or friend—to point out the error of their ways. Corey Pavin had a super 1991 season on the PGA Tour, and his good play came after he had reevaluated his life and judged that he had been pouring too much of himself into his golf career. Pavin converted from Judaism to Christianity and, like several other tour players, used his religion as a support base. Pavin also has a child, as do many of his peers, and they are also a good source for perspective. He regained a healthy perspective on golf and his game improved.

Also in 1991, Payne Stewart was bothered with a potential career-threatening nerve injury in his neck which sapped the muscle strength in his left arm. Rather than feel sorry for himself, Stewart worked hard on the mental side of the game during his recuperation, and a few months after being in a neck brace, he won the U.S. Open at Hazeltine National in Minnesota. The injury provided Stewart with some scary moments, but it also afforded him the chance to recognize how lucky he was to be a talented golfer.

While tour professionals have some reason to become obsessed with their games—it is their livelihood, after all—club golfers don't have the same excuse. People who allow a lousy round of golf to ruin their weekend or even their entire vacation need to take a hard look in the mirror. If you allow the game to affect you in this manner, work hard to change your attitude or you should consider giving up golf. It is simply not worth such heartache.

Having been fortunate enough to travel to Scotland a few times in recent years, it always does me good to see how much the Scots enjoy their golf while still holding a healthy perspective about it. Perhaps it is that they play without motorized carts on courses that aren't lined with real estate. They seem to play the game a little closer to nature, and it results in a wonderful outlook.

LEARNING FROM GOLF'S CHAMPIONS

While golf's greatest champions have thrilled us, entertained us, and inspired us throughout history, they also can serve an instructive purpose. Golf swings, equipment, and courses have changed greatly over the years, but the psychological makeup of the champions, all the way from old Tom Morris to Tom Watson, has changed very little.

All champions seem to possess the six traits described below. If any of the traits—even a portion of them—rubs off on your game, you're likely to see yourself improve. For the champions, the interaction of these six characteristics produces a mental makeup that makes them hard to beat.

PRESENCE

At peak performance, the best players have an aura which seems to intimidate lesser competitors. This aura could be seen in the eyes of Bobby Jones and Jack Nicklaus. Walter Hagen manifested it in his flamboyant behavior and dress. Ben Hogan's countenance was so intimidating to others that he was nicknamed "The Hawk." Arnold Palmer's magnetism with the galleries, and their support of him, unnerved many of his fellow players.

Whether the presence creates the champion or the champion creates the presence is a question of the chicken-egg type. It is also difficult to determine if a current player can dominate his fellow players for a sufficient period of time to establish this presence. As the 1992 season unfolded, it appeared that Fred Couples, whose Masters victory capped an amazing early-season record, was on the cusp of separating his free-flowing, powerful game from the rest of the pack. Only time will tell. Just a couple of years earlier, Seve Ballesteros and Greg Norman both seemed to be the most likely candidates to dominate today's game.

AROUSAL EQUALS POSITIVE ENERGY

In major championships, where the elite truly establish their reputations, there exists a higher level of arousal than in other events. Many lesser golfers are paralyzed by this arousal level and have virtually no chance of winning the big one. The champion, on the other hand, manages to use the arousal to energize his game and raise it to a higher plane. Increased tension leads to distress for most players, but for the champion it leads to eustress, a heightened level of awareness that seems to focus attention more acutely on the task at hand. The more important the shot, the more the champion seems to be able to tune in to his swing and disregard the distractions around him. In golf, champions persist despite golf's year-round calendar with weeks-long gaps between the major tournaments.

AN INTRINSIC LOVE FOR THE GAME

Golf's champions always have shown an intrinsic love and respect for the game. Prize money sufficient to support a player's family is a fairly recent phenomenon. Earlier champions had to work as club pros in order to support their play on the pro circuit. They didn't play solely for the money, nor do today's best golfers, despite the lucrative returns. Pro golfers rarely miss practicing or playing more than a couple of weeks per year. They're the rare pro athletes who will choose on their days off to play their sport with friends. Even with the knowledge that he would never play competitively again, Ben Hogan hit balls nearly every day out of love and a fascination for the game. Such a feeling for the sport is partly why Hogan was able to be such a dominating golfer in his prime.

RELAXED INTENSITY

This oxymoron works to explain how champions play. Jones and Byron Nelson, for example, had fluid swings which seemed to epitomize a relaxed nature. Yet both golfers were so intense on the inside that they suffered severe nervous reactions prior to championship play. Despite their affliction, both were able to calm themselves enough to focus on winning at the highest level. The champion must be relaxed enough to allow his body to produce the shots it has been trained to execute, but intense enough to prevent sloppy errors of indifference or inadequate forethought. Champions achieve this mix of relaxation and intensity in different ways. Hagen and Lee Trevino relaxed themselves by chatting with, and playing to, the spectators, while Hogan used his tunnel vision and inner-centeredness. Each champion learned to understand himself well enough to adapt his playing patterns to fit his personality. Trevino could not have been like Hogan, and vice versa.

LOVE OF COMPETITION

When the title is on the line, great players step forward, while lesser competitors shrink from the moment. This is true in all sports, and champion golfers have always "wanted the ball" in tight situations. They view competition as the ultimate measure of their performance, and they seek a higher standard against which they can compare their ability. Nicklaus frequently has said that all he ever wants is to be "in the hunt" on the last nine holes of the final round.

Love of competition doesn't mean that the champions always win. But it does mean that they seek the chance to be in a position to win or lose based on their ability. Perhaps this is why some of the most gracious losers in golf have been among the greatest champions. Listening to the champions talk, you sense that it is not so much "the thrill of victory" that motivates them as "the thrill of competition." This seemed evident at the memorable 1977 British Open Championship, when Watson edged Nicklaus in a remarkable display of golf by both men over the final two days. During play, Nicklaus remarked to Watson that such a competitive occasion was what the top golfers lived for.

COMMITMENT TO A POSITIVE COURSE OF ACTION

On and off the course, champions are very positive people. In many cases, this self-assuredness borders on cockiness or arrogance. Of one great champion, it was said, "He may be wrong, but he is never in doubt." Champions learn from their mistakes but they don't dwell on the negatives in any situation. They think about what they can do, not what they shouldn't do. Under pressure, they become aggressive while their opponents become passive. This isn't an artificial cockiness, but the inner self-assuredness of someone who has produced when all the chips were on the table.

APPLYING LESSONS FROM GOLF TO DAILY LIFE

You don't need me to tell you how beneficial golf can be to your well-being, do you? Especially not after you've just returned from a pleasant round with convivial friends on the kind of sunny spring day that should be patented. But golf can do more than you might imagine to your mental health: a round of golf can allow you to gain perspective on your problems and leave you mentally refreshed and ready to attack your worries with renewed vigor.

Golf's predictable structure is both comforting and relaxing. If you have a regular game, you can probably predict to the word what your partners will say on the first tee when they're setting up the sides and wagers. This predictability provides a safe harbor from some of the storms of the everyday world. Golf fills your mind, and the mental tribulations in your real life are put on hold. Errant drives, pulled irons, and jabbed putts are suddenly important matters. The beauty of golf courses—even your overgolfed muni is more attractive than you might think—and the leisurely pace of the game can put serenity in your life. Beyond these therapeutic benefits, there are at least seven mental-health skills or strategies that can be learned directly from golf and transferred to your daily life.

1. Live in the present tense. In order to be successful, golfers have to learn the inherent danger to their scorecard if they spend too much time worrying about a stroke they've just played or one which they're about to play. Sure, you have to learn from your mistakes and prepare for the future, but in golf, as in life, the only shot you can play is the one you're about to hit.

2. Develop a realistic locus of control. In psychological terms, *locus of control* relates to whether people perceive that they control their environment and the people and events in their lives (internal control) or are controlled by aspects of their environment (external control). In golf and in life, there are some things we can control but many others we realistically cannot. The important point is to figure out the difference. On the putting green, for instance, luck and chance play a big role in whether a putt is made. But you still owe it to yourself to take the time to read the green to the best of your ability, concentrate as well as possible, and put your best stroke on the ball. As in life, you need to control those factors you can control, acknowledge those you cannot, and have the wisdom to know the difference.

3. Adapt your behavior to fit the current situation. Frequently in golf you are subjected to slow play or to the idiosyncratic ways of your playing partners. You have to adapt to those variables or face a drop-off in performance. Off the course, you also need to be flexible and adaptable. This is very important as you age and might find yourself at odds with the younger generation's way of doing things. Rest assured, though, that you can be adaptable and flexible without sacrificing principle.

4. Develop self-analysis and self-understanding. As discussed earlier in this book, golfers must understand their personalities in order to figure out the best way for them to approach the learning and playing of the game.

Improvement seldom occurs until you learn to understand yourself. Are you an impulsive or a reflective decision-maker? Does your temper interfere with your game? Do you plan your way around the course, or do you make lots of strategic errors? Do you become easily distracted, allowing outside factors to interfere with your concentration or shotmaking? Successful businesspeople, professional persons, or pro athletes prosper largely because they learn to analyze their strengths and weaknesses, emphasizing the former and and minimizing the latter. Many times, people procrastinate in developing these traits off the course. But golf is relentless in demanding these skills if you are to improve.

5. Develop the skill of cognitive restructuring. With all the hazards to negotiate on the course, from sand bunkers to creeks to out-of-bounds stakes, you can choose to magnify these trouble spots or restructure the shot cognitively and "see" only the safe landing areas. How you choose to interpret what you "see" has much to do with the outcome of your shot.

Say a tour player misses the cut for two straight tournaments. Does he interpret this as a sign that he is headed for a prolonged slump, or does he restructure the situation and see it as a temporary condition that will help him because he is tired and the weekends off will give him some rest? It is the classic half-full/half-empty conundrum. What you learn in golf can transfer very well to everyday life, allowing you the chance to coach yourself positively through business decisions, public speaking presentations, and family or peer relationships.

6. Learn to accept yourself. Many golfers never learn how to forgive themselves for a misplayed shot. They let the mistake haunt them for the rest of the day, and it causes them to make other mistakes. But you need to accept your imperfections, learn from your mistakes, and focus on the next shot, or life task, without expending valuable psychic energy berating or criticizing yourself. Some psychological research indicates that people who cannot accept themselves have a very hard time accepting other people. If you learn to become more self-accepting and self-forgiving, you will improve your game and probably your relations with others as well.

7. Develop the wisdom to value the basics. The longer you play golf, the more you come to realize that in order to be successful, you have to value the basics. Fundamentals such as grip, posture, stance, and alignment might be boring things to practice—compared to some new swing theory on how to set the club at the top of the swing— but they are crucial to good shots. Transferring this philosophy to life, the fundamental things like family, friends, and relationships built on integrity are what really matter. Whether on or off the course, the person with integrity is the winner.

CHAPTER SUMMARY

- Be honest about how you play the game and realistic about the types of shots you are capable of hitting. Many amateurs try to pull off shots that tour pros wouldn't even try.
- Get to know how you think around the course. Figure out how missed short putts or hitting a ball out of bounds

affects your performance. Chart your scorecards to determine consistent scoring patterns.

- Enjoy golf, but avoid becoming obsessed with it. Even for tour professionals, golf should only be a part of their lives.
- Learn from golf's champions, who tend to enjoy psychological traits ranging from improved performance under pressure to a consistently positive outlook.
- Let lessons learned in golf transfer to your daily life. Golf teaches many things that are relevant in life, from living in the present to learning to accept yourself. Take advantage of the education.

APPENDIX: DISCOVERING YOUR GOLF PROFILE

As I said earlier in the book, I've learned something from each one of the hundreds of golfers of all handicap levels that I've helped with the mental side of golf. Among the most helpful and useful parts of my education have been the responses of golfers of all ability levels to the twenty-five questions that follow.

As you answer this golfing profile, be honest with yourself. The section following the questions will help you use your answers to the profile in a diagnostic way. It can help you figure out the aspects of your game that need the most attention and suggest ways to make productive changes in the way you approach your game.

1. Which part of the game do you practice most?
A. Driver
B. Fairway woods
C. Long irons
D. Middle irons
E. Short irons
F. Chipping
G. Putting
H. Sand shots
I. Other (Specify)

2. How many hours do you practice each week during the golf season?
A. Less than one hour

B. One to three hours
C. Four to six hours
D. Seven to ten hours
E. More than ten hours

3. In which of these situations are you concerned with how your swing and playing ability are perceived by others? Note each one that applies.
A. On the first tee with a crowd of onlookers
B. When invited to play with another foursome
C. When invited to play with much more skillful golfers
D. When you find that your teaching pro is watching you
E. Other situations (Specify)
F. I'm never concerned with what other people think of my golf game

4. How frequently do you visualize the flight of your shots before you swing?
A. Often
B. Occasionally
C. Rarely
D. Never

5. What pace of play do you generally like?
A. Rather quick
B. Moderate
C. Deliberate

6. How would you react to a slow foursome in

front of you on the course that won't let your group play through?

A. No problem. I would slow down my own pace, enjoy the scenery, or tell jokes between shots.

B. It would upset me some and might even have a temporary negative effect on my game.

C. It would upset me considerably and have a marked negative effect on my game. If I got even half a chance, I would ask them to let me play through.

D. It would drive me bananas. I couldn't handle it and would probably quit and go in.

7. Do you have one club that you're certain you will always hit well?

A. Yes

B. No

8. If a magic golf godmother could wave her wand and give you any golf skill or characteristic, which two of the following would you choose?

A. More distance off the tee

B. More accurate short irons

C. Better putting

D. Better sand play

E. Better long irons

F. More control over my emotions

G. Better concentration

H. Other (Specify)

9. Is there one hole on your home course that you consistently play poorly?

A. Yes (Specify how you feel when playing this hole.)

B. No   sinking apprehension

10. Is there one hole on your home course that you consistently play well? *Elated*
A. Yes (Specify how you feel when playing this hole.)
B. No

11. Which two of the following factors do you think contribute most to your poorly hit shots?
A. Lack of confidence
B. Lack of physical ability
C. Bad lies
D. Lack of knowledge of how to play the shot correctly
E. Lack of concentration
F. Fear
G. Factors such as water, sand, or out of bounds
H. Other (Specify)

12. Do you have a number of different mental cues or swing images you find helpful in playing certain kinds of shots?
A. Yes (Specify)
B. No

13. What is your single greatest psychological fear when playing golf?
A. Playing out of sand
B. Hitting a bad shot off the first tee when people are watching
C. Missing short putts
D. Hitting shots over water
E. Hitting shots out of bounds on tight holes
F. Playing with golfers much better than I am

G. Shanking

H. Other (Specify)

14. Do you have a specific routine to warm up physically before a round (things such as stretching exercises, practice swings, or hitting practice balls)?

A. Yes

B. No

15. Do you have a specific routine to psychologically prepare yourself to play, such as rehearsing swing images or cues, or doing relaxation exercises?

A. Yes

B. No

16. When preparing to putt, how often do you clearly see "a line extending from your ball to the cup" as if someone had painted the line with a brush and paint?

A. Never

B. Rarely

C. Sometimes

D. Frequently

E. What do you think I am, crazy?

17. Is there a particular stretch of holes (first two holes, last three holes, holes five through eight, etc.) that you consistently play well?

A. Yes

B. No

18. Is there a stretch of holes that you consistently play poorly?
A. Yes
B. No

19. How often do you practice your preswing alignment by putting down clubs parallel to your swing line or by asking a friend to check your alignment and setup for you?
A. Frequently
B. Sometimes
C. Rarely
D. Never

20. Have you ever played golf with someone who had a herky-jerky swing and found that you began to lose your rhythm and tempo after a few holes?
A. Yes
B. No

21. If you feel you are losing your swing rhythm or tempo, do you have someone with whom you seek to play a round of golf so that by observing his swing tempo you might regain your own?
A. Yes
B. No

22. If you hit two or three poor shots in a row, what are your thoughts just before setting up to play your next shot?
A. I feel very confident since every shot must be played one at a time.

B. I have a vague fear of not hitting the ball well.
C. I am extremely apprehensive and fearful of mishitting the shot.
D. I just hope that I somehow can get the ball airborne.

23. Do you have a particular range of scores (such as 75—80, 85—90, 95—100) that you feel comfortable shooting?
A. Yes (Specify your comfort zone.) 116 — 120
B. No

24. How much impact on your total self-concept does your golf skill have?
A. None at all; I forget my game as soon as I leave the course.
B. Very little; I remember the game for a short while, then put it out of my mind.
C. A moderate impact, but other things are more important.
D. A tremendous impact; it is quite important to my overall self-concept.

25. How closely does your golf self-concept match the self-concept you have off the course?
A. They are identical.
B. They are rather close but not the same.
C. They are quite different.
D. They are exact opposites.

To start analyzing your golfing profile, first consider how you answered questions 1 and 8, which ask you

(1) which part of the game you practice the most, and (2) which golf skill you would most like to have. Extremely high handicappers notwithstanding, most golfers respond that they would like to putt better, yet none of the handicap groups say that they spend most of their practice time on the putting green. Putting, in fact, was practiced very little. Tour professionals, however, say that they spend most of their practice time on the green, indicating that unlike amateurs, they aren't afraid to work on their weaknesses.

About question 2, on the amount of practice time, better players say they practice more than poor players. For example, 11 percent of single-digit handicappers practiced seven to ten hours per week; no golfer with a handicap of 24 or higher said he practiced that much.

3. Higher handicappers are much more concerned with how their swing and ability are perceived by others on the first tee or when they're asked to play with strangers or players much more skilled than themselves. Low-handicap golfers are more concerned when they see their teaching pro watching them. For everyone, however, the only way to be comfortable in any of these situations is to be put in them repeatedly. When that becomes the case, you'll find yourself thinking about your swing—and your game—and not about who is watching you.

4. Lower-handicap players are much more likely to visualize shots before hitting them. Better golfers also see the line to the cup more frequently when putting (question 16). If you're not visualizing your shots, your teaching pro may be able to help you.

Questions 5 and 6 are related and it probably comes as no surprise to you that as a fact of human nature, golfers who say they prefer to play quickly often say they have a tough time adjusting to a slow group ahead of them on the course.

7. If you said that you have a favorite club you tend to hit well all the time, think about how you feel when you have this club in your hand. Most people report they are relaxed, confident, and not worried about an off-line shot. It would be nice to feel this way about all your clubs, right? Well, check to see which clubs you practice the most—chances are, your favorites are the ones you practice the most.

Questions 9 and 10 address the holes that you consistently play poorly or well. You may play holes poorly because of physical or mechanical reasons. The hole may dogleg from right to left, and your normal shot might be a fade or slice. You might not have the length to reach another hole in regulation. If you have either of these problems, work to correct them. Try to learn to move the ball in the other direction; become more flexible or stronger to gain distance off the tee; or practice your short-game skills so that you can get up and down for par on the long holes you can't reach in regulation.

You may be playing holes badly for psychological reasons (questions 11 and 13). If this is true for you, figure out the stimuli that cause you the most concern, whether they are out-of-bounds stakes, water hazards, or sand bunkers. If it's possible, venture out early in the morning or late in the afternoon and play your nemesis holes over and over. See yourself hitting good shots on these holes, and savor them, storing them in your memory so you can recall these successes when you face the hole for real the next time.

In question 12, better players indicate they rely on

mental cues or images when playing certain shots; poorer golfers rarely do. Good golfers learn to cue up a particular move in their swing that enables them to hit a certain type of shot. When they're playing at the highest level, most tour players use cues and images, not mechanical thoughts.

To encourage golfers to store up their "swing feel" in in terms of cues and images, I ask students to keep a small notebook in their golf bag, with pages devoted to each type of club. When the student has a particularly good day with a specific club, he jots down in the notebook exactly how he felt when he hit it. Then, when he starts having trouble hitting a certain club, he has a written record instead of a vague memory to assist in regaining his swing sense.

Questions 14 and 15 address mental and physical preparation before each round. While most golfers surveyed say they have some form of physical warm-up before playing, only the very best say they follow a preround routine to prepare them psychologically. For example, how many times have you practiced early in the week and discovered a swing key that worked very well? You tell yourself that this thought is going to make your Saturday round of golf go well. But when the weekend rolls around, you rush to the course and forget the swing thought until well into your round—by then, your score and your mood are shot.

To avoid this trap, use the principles described in chapter 5, keeping in mind that the purpose of a preround warm-up is to arrive at the first tee in a playing, rather than a ball-bashing, mode.

Questions 17 and 18 concern patterns of good and bad play. You can figure out your play patterns by breaking down each round into six three-hole sets. You'll probably discover that a particular set (or sets) consistently has higher scores because of where the holes fall during the round. Your problem could be as straightforward as that of a tour player I once worked with. When this player figured out his play patterns, he found that the thirteenth, fourteenth, and fifteenth holes, regardless of the course, were where he had trouble. The problem turned out to be his poor diet, which caused his energy to wane at that point in the round. In turn, his concentration slipped and his scores went up. A better diet, including appropriate on-course nutrition, solved the problem.

For question 19, about alignment, good players indicate that they spend much more time practicing alignment using visual aids or with help from friends or their teacher than do poor players. Poorer golfers say they work hard at building a swing but spend little time on alignment. If this sounds like you, work more on the preswing variables, as the better players do.

Questions 20 and 21 ask how you're affected by observing the swing rhythm of others. Many more feel-oriented golfers seem to be affected than analytical players. If watching others causes you problems, avoid doing it. Conversely, if you've found that you make better swings after observing a sweet swinger, you should make a point to watch him.

If you checked answer C or D to question 22, you need to learn to play one shot at a time, without regard to previous shots. The better the golfer, the more frequently answer A was chosen. Better players analyze their poor shots, but they don't lose their confidence when they step up to the next shot. They also tend to remain cool and somewhat detached and they avoid blaming themselves.

In answering question 23, golfers of all abilities indicate they have a scoring comfort zone and they find ways to give back shots until they return to their zone. Two strategies can help you become comfortable in a lower scoring zone. First, play a round without any scoring expectations. Think about how well you have played when you were a little sick or injured, or on the first round back after a long winter layoff. Second, try to "get lost in shotmaking." Players have reported shooting career rounds in a mental fog; they didn't know how they stood in relation to par because they were so focused on each individual shot.

Finally, questions 24 and 25 ask how your golf game affects you as a person. Among those who've filled out the profile, the results indicate that golfing skill has a greater impact on total self-concept for higher handicappers than for better golfers. This may mean that bad play can make people have negative self-perceptions but that good play doesn't have much impact on positive self-feelings. For the health of your game, and yourself overall, keep things in perspective regardless of your handicap. This will not only help you to be a better golfer but it will also help you be a better person off the course.

INDEX